First published 2024

(c) 2024 Dominic Salles

All rights reserved. The right of Dominic Salles to be identified as th been asserted by them in accordance with the Copyright, Designs a... ...ents Act 1988. No part of this work may be reproduced, stored in a retrieval system, transmitted in any form or by any means, electronical, mechanical, photocopying, recording, or otherwise, without the prior permission of the Author.

Dominic Salles still lives in Swindon, with his workaholic wife Deirdre. His jiu-jitsu-loving ex-engineer son, Harry, has moved to Shoreditch and lives on the site of Shakespeare's first theatre, The Curtain. Destiny. For those of you who remember Bob, he is now an ex-dog. It is curtains for him also.

His daughter Jess has just moved to New Zealand where the surf is better and schools are more fun.

His sister Jacey is an actress, famous for her Spanish accent, on your TV screens in shows like Casualty and Cold Feet. She would be hilarious in her own YouTube channel. Tweet her to let her know.

His YouTube channel, Mr Salles Teaches English, has reached 131,000 subscribers and had over 25 million views, about which he is childishly excited. 77% of his viewers reported getting grades 7-9.

He drives a Toyota Prius and has installed solar panels this year to offset his enormous carbon footprint.

Other Grade 9 Guides by Mr Salles

Language
The Mr Salles Guide to **100% at AQA GCSE English Language**
The Mr Salles Guide to **Awesome Story Writing**
The Mr Salles Quick Guide to **Awesome Description**
The Mr Salles **Ultimate Guide to Description**
The Mr Salles Quick **Guide to Grammar, Punctuation and Spelling**
The Mr Salles **Ultimate Guide to Persuasive Writing**
The Mr Salles Guide to 100% in AQA GCSE **English Language Paper 1 Question 2**
The Mr Salles Guide to 100% in AQA GCSE **English Language Paper 1 Question 3**
The Mr Salles Guide to 100% in AQA GCSE **English Language Paper 1 Question 4**

The Mr Salles Guide to 100% in AQA GCSE **English Language Paper 1 Question 5**
The Mr Salles Guide to 100% in AQA GCSE **English Language Paper 2 Question 2**
The Mr Salles Guide to 100% in AQA GCSE **English Language Paper 2 Question 3**
20 Top Grade GCSE Story Plots: Boost Your Grade with the Secrets of Structure

Literature
The Mr Salles Guide to **GCSE English Literature**
Study Guide Mr Salles Analyses **Jekyll and Hyde**
The Mr Salles Ultimate Guide to **Macbeth**
The Mr Salles Guide to **An Inspector Calls**
The Mr Salles Ultimate Guide to **A Christmas Carol**
The Mr Salles Ultimate Guide to **Romeo and Juliet**
Mr Salles **Power and Conflict** Top Grade Essay Guide (AQA Anthology): 11 Grade 9 Exam Essays!

Books on Teaching

The Full English: How to be a brilliant English teacher
The Slightly Awesome Teacher: Using Edu-research to get brilliant results
The Unofficial Ofsted Survival Guide
Differentiate Your School: where every student learns more

Contents

Other Grade 9 Guides by Mr Salles 1
Books on Teaching 2
Starting With the Extract 6
  Grades 1-7 6
  Grades 8 and 9 7
  I Just Want to Start With the Extract 7
This is what the marks mean as a percentage: 8
  What Do the Marking Criteria Mean? 9
  Let's look at what students actually *do* to get marks in each level. 9
  Grade 9 10
  On Average, What do Students Do for Each Grade? 10
  What You Should Aim For 11
How to Plan Your Essay for Top Grades 12
What if This Contradicts My Teacher's Advice? 13
Ok, most teachers won't have read and analysed dozens of answers marked by senior examiners. And if they have, most won't have tried to break them down into the skills I have looked at. 13
  Question 1 15
    Based on June 2019 15
  3 Minute Plan 16
  Based on November 2020 17
  3 Minute Plan 18
  Based on November 2021 20
  3 Minute Plan 21
  Based on June 2018 23
    Read this extract from Act 1 Scene 3. 23
    Answer the question that follows. 23
  3 Minute Plan 24
  8 Skills of Essay Writing 25
Simple, explicit comments   1–5 marks Grade 1 26
  Question 1 27
  Response 1 27
  Question 4 29
  Response 2 29
  Question 2 30
  Response 3 30

Question 4	32
Response 4	32

Supported, relevant comments   6–10 marks Grade 2 34

Question 2	34
Response 5	34

Explained, structured comments   11–15 marks Grade 3 - 4 36

Question 2	36
Response 6	36
Question 1	39
Response 7	39
Question 2	41
Response 8	41

Clear understanding 43
16–20 marks Grades 5 and 6 43

Question 1	43
Response 9	43
Question 3	46
Response 10	46
Question 2	48
Response 11	48
Question 3	51
Response 12	51
Question 1	54
Response 13	54

Thoughtful, developed consideration   21–25 marks Grades 7 and 8 57

Question 3	57
Response 14	57
Question 4	60
Response 15	60
Question 1	63
Response 16	63
Question 1	66
Response 17	66

Convincing, critical analysis and exploration   26–30 marks Grade 9 69

Question 2	69
Response 18	69

Question 1	73
Response 19	73
Question 1	76
Response 20	76
Question 4	80
Response 21	80
Question 3	84
Response 22	84
How does Shakespeare present Macbeth's fears?	87
Response 23	87
How does Shakespeare present the theme of ambition in the play?	90
Response 24	90
How Does Shakespeare Present the Supernatural in Macbeth?	93
Response 25	93
My Final Version Combining ChatGPT Paragraphs	97
Response 26	97

Introduction

There are 4 questions you probably have about the Macbeth extract question:

1. What do I need to know to get the grade I want?
2. How do I structure my answer to get that grade?
3. How can I get a higher grade?
4. What does a grade 9 answer look like?

If so, this is exactly the guide you want.

The answer to those questions also changes if you want to get higher than a grade 7.

I hope you will also have another question:

5. I find it hard to see what you mean when you explain it. Can you just show me?

That's where the real magic happens. By seeing actual essays – not just sample paragraphs, but full answers – at every single grade, you will understand *exactly* how to improve your writing.

You will understand exactly what will get you the grade you want.

Starting With the Extract

You don't have to start with the extract. Nothing in the mark scheme tells you to do that.

> **Student**: Ah, but the question tells you to write 'starting with the extract'. If you don't, isn't that a 'rubric infringement'?
>
> **Mr Salles**: This is what AQA says in the mark scheme. It is a rubric infringement if the answer is not a "response to extract and whole text".
>
> **Student**: So, as long as I write about the whole text and the extract, I'm fine. I can do it in any order?
>
> **Mr Salles**: Exactly.

Grades 1-7

Every essay in this guide starts with the extract. There are two reasons for this.

1. Every essay AQA publish starts with the extract.

2. I use this to show you exactly how starting with the extract *cost the student marks and grades*.

Starting with the extract will get you lower grades. You will get higher grades if you work through the play in the order in which things happen. So, work through the play chronologically.

Why? Because the second half of the question is to write about the "whole play".

So, you need something about the beginning, middle and end of the play. You might not manage that by starting with the extract.

But you will ***always*** manage it if you work through the play chronologically.

Grades 8 and 9

If you are a hard working student, and not one of the cleverest students in your class, you can still get grades 8 and 9.

- Don't start with the extract. Work through the play chronologically.
- Write as fast as you can.

If you are one of the smartest students in your class.

- Start with the extract if you want.
- Keep writing about the extract with lots of interpretations and context to back up your ideas.
- Write as fast as you can.

I Just Want to Start With the Extract

No problem. Here are 25 essays to show you how to do that at each grade.

For each essay you get senior examiner comments telling you why it got the grade. And you get my comments showing you how to improve the grade.

Mark Scheme at a Glance

Grade 9	Marks	Criteria	Level
9	26	**Convincing**, critical analysis and exploration	Level 6 26–30 marks
8	24	**Thoughtful**, developed consideration	Level 5 21–25 marks
7	21		
6	18	**Clear** understanding	Level 4 16–20 marks
5	16		
4	13	**Explained**, structured comments	Level 3 11–15 marks
3	11		

- The first column is whatever grade you are after. No one reading this guide wants a grade 2 or 1, so I left those out.

- The second column tells you the first mark which gets the grade. All the marks are out of 30. So, grade 7 starts at 21 marks, and stops at 23.

- The third column tells you how to decide on your gut reaction about an answer, as soon as you have read it. That's what examiners do.

- The final column tells you what level it is in the mark scheme. Exam boards can't publish grades in the mark scheme, because grade boundaries move every year.

This is what the marks mean as a percentage:

Grade 9   88%   =   26

Grade 8   79%   =   24

Grade 7   71%   =   21

Grade 6   61%   =   18

Grade 5   52%   =   16

Grade 4   43%   =   13

You only need just over 50% for a grade 5, and 60% for a grade 6.

Most students don't even get 60%. But you will smash it.

What Do the Marking Criteria Mean?

You can skip this – it's just me trying to show you why the marking criteria are really hard to understand, even for teachers and English examiners.

- What is an **explicit** comment?
- Why is that worse than a **relevant** comment?
- How is **supported** different from **explained**?
- How is **clear** better than **structured** – surely structured should be better than clear?
- What is **developed** in comparison to **clear**?
- How do I decide something is **thoughtful** or **thoughtful and convincing**?
- What is **consideration** compared to **exploration**?
- When does an **analysis** become **critical**, rather than just an analysis?

I could explain all of these to you, but the truth is nobody knows for sure. We are all just making our best guess.

And, even if every English teacher agreed with my explanations, these wouldn't tell you *how* to actually write an answer.

Marking criteria are nowhere near as helpful as seeing what students actually *do* to get the marks.

Let's look at what students actually *do* to get marks in each level.

You don't have to read this table, so I'll explain it and you can decide if it is useful.
Let's read the top row and then see what I say about it at the bottom of the table:

Level	Words	Thesis	Exp.	Quote	Methods	Context	Shake	Exp L	Conc.	Para
6	975	Y	22	13	8	9	9	3	Y	9
5	760	Y	18	9	4	6	4	3	Y	7
4	583	Y	10	10	2	3	1	1	Y	7
3	521	N	11	4	1	2	3	1	Y	5
2	256	N	5	3	0	1	4	0	N	4
1	184	N	2	4	0	0	1	0	N	3

There are 11 columns. This is what they all mean:

9

Grade 9

1. **Level 6** you might remember is grade 9.
2. On average, grade 9 students wrote 975 **words**.
3. They all started their essay with a **thesis** statement.
4. On average, they wrote at least 22 **explanations** to quotes.
5. On average they used 13 different **quotes**.
6. They didn't **name a method** for each quote. They named 8 methods on average.
7. They used **context** (stuff about the time the play was written) 9 times.
8. To explain **Shakespeare**'s ideas, they used his **name** 9 times.
9. They used **exploratory language** (words like could, might, may, probably) 3 times.
10. They all wrote a **conclusion**.
11. There were 9 **paragraphs**, so they averaged over 97 words each paragraph.

On Average, What do Students Do for Each Grade?

Grade 4
- Write about 1.5 to 2 pages of A4, which is about 450 - 550 words.
- You can do it with a lot less. But students at grade 4 are not good writers, and use lots and lots words to explain simple ideas.
- Write 5 paragraphs.
- Write about at least 4 quotes – at least one from the rest of the play.
- Mention the views of the Jacobean audience and King James.
- Write about 1 method if you can – use words like **symbol, metaphor, simile, contrast**.

Grade 5
- All of the grade 4 stuff, just better.

Grade 6
- Write a thesis statement in which you explain Shakespeare's viewpoint about the topic of the question
- Write 550 – 650 words, so 2 – 2.5 pages of A4.
- Include 10 quotes.
- Write 10 explanations about them.
- Name 2 methods
- Refer to any of Jacobean audience, King James, the Great Chain of Being etc 3 times to back up your explanations.
- Write 7 paragraphs.

Grade 7
- All of grade 6, but:
- Write 700-800 words
- Have 18 explanations
- And 9 or 10 quotes (which tells you that you must write nearly 2 explanations for each quote)
- Name 4 methods – so one for every second quote
- Use context 6 times to back up your explanations: Daemonologie, divine right of kings, iambic pentameter, tragedy get added to your list.
- Mention Shakespeare 4 times, but make sure to refer to his ideas and purpose each time.

Grade 8
- The same as grade 7 but better.

Grade 9
- See above

What You Should Aim For

Whatever your grade is at the minute, you can aim for all of these:
1. Write a thesis statement.
2. Write a conclusion.
3. The more you write, the higher your mark will be. Quantity is more important than quality (though some students at grade 8 and 9 get away with less)
4. Use as many quotes as you can.
5. When you spot a method, state what it is. If you can't spot a method, call it 'imagery'.
6. If you can, write two explanations per quote, so at least some of them will have more than one explanation.
7. The more you write about Shakespeare's point of view with your explanations, the higher your mark will be.
8. To back up your ideas, use any context which is relevant.

Make it Even More Simple
1. Write as much as you can – 750 to 1200 words if you are able.
2. Have 10-15 quotes. This will mean 5 – 10 which are not in the extract.
3. Write a thesis statement and a conclusion.
4. Always write about Shakespeare's purpose.
5. Use context to help you write about his purpose.

How to Plan Your Essay for Top Grades

Step 1
Start with a 3 point thesis statement. This is easy to do in advance, because Shakespeare's purpose remains the same, whatever the question:

1. Macbeth is a cautionary tale, warning any rebellious nobles about the consequences of regicide, particularly following the gunpowder plot.
2. The supernatural is introduced in order to please King James, his patron, and to play on the contemporary fear of witches.
3. The violence, madness and death of Lady Macbeth and Macbeth are divine punishment for committing regicide and attacking the Great Chain of Being.
4. The play is a tragedy, exploring the hamartia and downfall of a great man destroyed by his own ambition.
5. Lady Macbeth represents either the misogynistic view that women are, like Eve, evil temptresses or the damaging effects of patriarchal control of women.
6. The play explores the theme of kingship both in order to celebrate King James' noble ancestry, and also as a cautionary tale in order to teach King James not to persecute Catholics and the nobles he suspects might have aided the plotters.

You would pick which 2 or 3 fit your essay. Most students don't pick any at all.

Example:

Let's imagine the question is on the supernatural. I can combine points 1 and 2 above.

Shakespeare includes the supernatural as **to warn the nobles at court that regicide is an act against God, fundamentally evil** *and, like the gunpowder plot, likely to fail.* **He focuses on the witches in particular in order to flatter King James**, his patron who wrote Daemonologie about witchcraft, and **to play on the Jacobean fear of witches**.

Annoyingly this is a four part thesis. When I was thinking about the 'consequences' in point 1, I wrote down the idea in italics.

You can combine any of the ideas above in any combination – I just chose the first 2.

Step 2
Spend 3 minutes writing a chronological plan. Pick 6 events which are relevant to the title, and quote from these to develop your argument.

Also write down any concepts and context you know will fit – The Great Chain of Being, Daemonologie, Divine Right of Kings, prose and iambic pentameter, Machiavellian ...

Step 3
Work through the play chronologically, so that you can build an argument in answer to your thesis.

Step 4
Deal with the extract as one of those 6 events, in the right chronological order. These might be 6 separate paragraphs.

Step 5
Write a conclusion which looks at Shakespeare's final point of view about the topic of the essay.

This gives you an 8 paragraph essay which is going to get grades 7-9.

This method will add at least a grade, possibly two grades, to all the grade 1 – 8 essays in this guide, because they just started with the extract.

You can totally ignore this if you already write about the extract so well that you are getting 26-30 out of 30.

There are 6 answers like this you can learn from. And another 2 which follow my advice for beyond grade 9 answers.

How to Plan for Grades 5 and 6
Do what you can from the list above.

- This might be 1 idea from Step 1, maybe 2.
- 1 more idea from Step 1.
- All of Step 3.
- All of Step 5.
- Step 6 – write a conclusion in which you refer back to the idea in Step 1.
- Take 5 minutes to do it, instead of 3.

What if This Contradicts My Teacher's Advice?

Ok, most teachers won't have read and analysed dozens of answers marked by senior examiners. And if they have, most won't have tried to break them down into the skills I have looked at.

So, let's be honest, my advice is definitely going to be slightly different, and sometimes very different to your teacher.

Read the student answers. **None** of my advice comes from what I believe. They are **all** things I have discovered from reading dozens of marked answers.

So, once you have read these marked answers, decide. Does my advice make sense or not? You might have a better idea, and spot something that I've missed. So might your teacher.

There is one other way you can use my advice. Ignore it. Read the essays which are at least the grade you want. Then write a new essay using whatever method you like.

If your teacher grades this at the grade you want, job done.

If not, go back to my advice.

The Questions and My 8 Point Plans

Quotes or References?

In the exam, my plan will be quick. I won't put in quotation marks. I probably won't put the whole quote – just enough to remind me which quote to use.

So here, I'll just put words from the quote in bold.

What happens if you don't remember the quote in the exam? Just a reference will do. It still counts.

Question 1

Based on June 2019

Read this extract from Act 1 Scene 2 of Macbeth.

Then answer the question that follows.

At this point in the play, the Captain tells Duncan about Macbeth's part in the recent battle against the Norwegian invaders.

CAPTAIN.
Doubtful it stood;
As two spent swimmers that do cling together
And choke their art. The merciless Macdonwald
(Worthy to be a rebel, for to that
The multiplying villainies of nature
Do swarm upon him) from the Western Isles
Of kerns and gallowglasses is supplied;
And Fortune, on his damned quarrel smiling,
Show'd like a rebel's whore. But all's too weak;
For brave Macbeth (well he deserves that name),
Disdaining Fortune, with his brandish'd steel,
Which smok'd with bloody execution,
Like Valour's minion, carv'd out his passage,
Till he fac'd the slave;
Which ne'er shook hands, nor bade farewell to him,
Till he unseam'd him from the nave to the chops,
And fix'd his head upon our battlements.

DUNCAN.
O valiant cousin! worthy gentleman!

Explore how far Shakespeare presents Macbeth as a violent character.

Start with this extract.

Write about:

- **how Shakespeare presents Macbeth in this extract**
- **how far Shakespeare presents Macbeth as a violent character in the play as a whole.**

3 Minute Plan

1. Thesis – attack on Jacobean masculinity, martial society, cautionary tale against regicide
2. Macbeth's enjoyment of violence – **unseamed**
3. His sick sense of humour – **shook hands**
4. His skill – **smoked with bloody execution**
5. His bloodlust is his hamartia– **horrid image … unfix my hair** at killing Duncan
6. How this leads to divine punishment of addiction, guilt, madness
7. His addiction – kills the grooms, when the plan was to keep them alive
8. His guilt – **never shake they gory locks … thou canst not say I did it**
9. His madness – **dagger I see before me … my mind is full of scorpions**
10. His self-destruction – his confession to killing Duncan – **I did it**
11. Killing Macduff's family leads to Macduff killing him – I'm **stepped in blood so deep**
12. Conclusion - Final judgement – **dead butcher** and **fiend-like queen**

Notice
- The extract will be covered in points 2, 3 and 4.
- The 6 further events are points 5, 7, 8, 9 (which is 2 connected events I'm treating as one), 11, 12
- They are all in chronological order
- I haven't written out full quotations, or used quotation marks, because I want my plan to be as quick as possible.

Question 2

Based on November 2020

Read this extract from Act 5 Scene 1 of Macbeth.

Then answer the question that follows.

At this point in the play, the Doctor and the Gentlewoman are watching Lady Macbeth, while she is sleepwalking.

LADY MACBETH.
Out, damned spot! out, I say! One; two. Why, then 'tis time to do't. Hell is murky! Fie, my lord, fie! a soldier, and afeard? What need we fear who knows it, when none can call our power to account? Yet who would have thought the old man to have had so much blood in him?

DOCTOR.
Do you mark that?

LADY MACBETH.
The Thane of Fife had a wife. Where is she now?—What, will these hands ne'er be clean? No more o' that, my lord, no more o' that: you mar all with this starting.

DOCTOR.
Go to, go to. You have known what you should not.

GENTLEWOMAN.
She has spoke what she should not, I am sure of that: heaven knows what she has known.

LADY MACBETH.
Here's the smell of the blood still: all the perfumes of Arabia will not sweeten this little hand. Oh, oh, oh!

DOCTOR.
What a sigh is there! The heart is sorely charged.

GENTLEWOMAN.
I would not have such a heart in my bosom for the dignity of the whole body.

DOCTOR.
Well, well, well.

GENTLEWOMAN.

Pray God it be, sir.

DOCTOR.

This disease is beyond my practice: yet I have known those which have walked in their sleep, who have died holily in their beds.

LADY MACBETH.

Wash your hands, put on your nightgown; look not so pale. I tell you yet again, Banquo's buried; he cannot come out on's grave.

DOCTOR.

Even so?

LADY MACBETH.

To bed, to bed. There's knocking at the gate. Come, come, come, come, give me your hand. What's done cannot be undone. To bed, to bed, to bed.

How far does Lady Macbeth change as a character and as a woman during the play.

Start with the extract.

Write about:

- **how Shakespeare presents Lady Macbeth in this extract**
- **how far Shakespeare presents Lady Macbeth as a woman who changes in the play as a whole.**

3 Minute Plan

1. Thesis: Shakespeare presents her as a powerful woman to explore misogynistic, patriarchal and religious oppression of women. Shows her decline is divine punishment for sin, perhaps Original Sin and perhaps link to supernatural evil. But Macbeth still loves her.
2. Understands her husband? - **Too full of the milk**
3. Masculine cruelty, supernatural – **unsex me here**
4. Emasculates Macbeth, control – **put this night's great business into my dispatch**
5. Again when he refuses – **coward, what beast**
6. Inhuman violence, grief at her own baby's death, failure to provide heir – **dashed his brains out**
7. Patriarchal control is deep – can't kill, as **looked like my father** – symbolism
8. Eventual madness triggered by – **give me the daggers**
9. Faints when Macbeth deviates from plan, killing grooms

10. Sleepwalking – **out damned spot** – fear of hell and link to blood
11. Guilt – **old man's blood**, link to her weakness
12. Fear of what she has unleashed in Macbeth – they sleep apart, **the Thane of Fife had a wife**
13. Suicide and Macbeth's reaction – **out, out, brief candle** echoing her language
14. Conclusion - **Fiend like queen** – just or unjust?

There are 8 events, plus the conclusion.

1. Points 2 and 3 occur together.
2. Points 4 and 5 go together.
3. Points 6
4. Point 7
5. Point 8
6. Point 9
7. Points 10, 11 and 12 occur together
8. Point 13

I've recommended 6 events as a way to plan your essay – so, I would get rid of the least important which are probably 6 and 9 from my 14 point list.

Question 3

Based on November 2021

Read this extract from Act 2 Scene 2 of Macbeth.

Then answer the question that follows.

At this point in the play, Macbeth has just killed Duncan. He has returned to Lady Macbeth.

MACBETH.
Methought I heard a voice cry, 'Sleep no more:
Macbeth does murder sleep', the innocent sleep,
Sleep that knits up the ravelled sleeve of care,
The death of each day's life, sore labour's bath,
Balm of hurt minds, great nature's second course,
Chief nourisher in life's feast.

LADY MACBETH.
What do you mean?

MACBETH.
Still it cried, 'Sleep no more' to all the house;
'Glamis hath murdered sleep', and therefore Cawdor
Shall sleep no more: Macbeth shall sleep no more.

LADY MACBETH
Who was it, that thus cried? Why, worthy thane,
You do unbend your noble strength to think
So brain-sickly of things. Go get some water
And wash this filthy witness from your hand.
Why did you bring these daggers from the place?
They must lie there. Go carry them and smear
The sleepy grooms with blood.

MACBETH
I'll go no more. I am afraid to think what I have done;
Look on't again, I dare not.

LADY MACBETH
Infirm of purpose!
Give me the daggers. The sleeping and the dead

Are but as pictures; 'tis the eye of childhood
That fears a painted devil. If he do bleed, I'll gild the faces of the grooms withal,
For it must seem their guilt.

How does Shakespeare present the relationship between Macbeth and Lady Macbeth?

Write about:

- **how Shakespeare presents their relationship in the extract from Act 2 Scene 2**
- **how Shakespeare presents the relationship between Macbeth and Lady Macbeth in the play as a whole.**

3 Minute Plan

1. Thesis: The patriarchal view presents Lady Macbeth as Machiavellian, serpent like, evil as the witches emasculating Macbeth. Alternatively, they are in love, Macbeth manipulates her and loves her even at the end.
2. The letter – **dearest partner of greatness**
3. Partnership – **put this night's great business**
4. Masculine roles – **unsex me here, direst cruelty, bring forth men-children only**
5. Joint grief over dead child – **dashed its brains out**
6. Belittles him, emasculates – **was the hope drunk, what beast, coward**
7. Covers for him, faints – **why did you so?***
8. Again at the feast – **my lord is often thus**
9. Macbeth protects her/excludes her – **be innocent of the knowledge**
10. His care for her on eve of battle – **canst thou not minister to a mind diseased**
11. Constant care for him revealed in sleepwalking – **what's done cannot be undone***
12. Love/indifference suggested by **out, out brief candle** – mirrors her language, symbolic of light.
13. He welcomes death once she is dead – **such a one am I to fear** – seeks him out
14. Conclusion – **dead butcher** and **fiend-like queen** – a partnership?

Again, I'm giving you more detail than I would give myself.

*This is a rare plan, where the extract is not one I would have chosen to answer the question. In this instance, I know I would be able to link the extract to Point 7 – Macbeth was supposed to follow the plan, but keeps failing to do so. And to Point 11 - she tries to soothe his mind here, and then relives similar moments when she sleepwalks.

If you couldn't do this, you would slot this scene in chronologically – it would therefore replace Point 7.

1. Points 2 and 3 are one event.

21

2. Point 4.
3. Points 5 and 6 are the same event.
4. Points 7 and 8 are separate moments, but the same thing, so I'm treating it as one event.
5. Points 9 and 10 are also separate moments, but the same thing.
6. Point 11.
7. Point 12.
8. Point 13.

Annoyingly, I need to get rid of 2 to limit myself to 6 for you! Obviously, you could write about all of these in the exam, but I am trying to stick to a 6 event limit to make planning easier for you.

Points 5 and 7 are the ones most students would not write about, so they are the easiest ones to get rid of.

Question 4

Based on June 2018

Read this extract from Act 1 Scene 3.

Answer the question that follows.

At this point in the play, Banquo and Macbeth have just met the witches and heard their prophecies.

BANQUO.
But 'tis strange;
And oftentimes, to win us to our harm,
The instruments of darkness tell us truths,
Win us with honest trifles, to betray's
In deepest consequence-
Cousins, a word, I pray you.

MACBETH. [Aside.]
Two truths are told,
As happy prologues to the swelling act
Of the imperial theme-I thank you, gentlemen.
[Aside.] This supernatural soliciting
Cannot be ill, cannot be good. If ill,
Why hath it given me earnest of success,
Commencing in a truth? I am Thane of Cawdor.
If good, why do I yield to that suggestion
Whose horrid image doth unfix my hair
And make my seated heart knock at my ribs,
Against the use of nature? Present fears
Are less than horrible imaginings:
My thought, whose murder yet is but fantastical,
Shakes so my single state of man that function
Is smothered in surmise, and nothing is
But what is not.

BANQUO.
Look, how our partner's rapt.

MACBETH. [Aside.]
If chance will have me King, why, chance may crown me
Without my stir.

Starting with this moment in the play explore how Shakespeare presents the attitude of Macbeth and Banquo towards the supernatural.

3 Minute Plan

Thesis: Shakespeare panders to King James' fascination – Daemonology – but also uses them as the Fates, simply with the gift of prophecy to show personal responsibility and Macbeth's Hamartia – cautionary tale. Banquo as antithesis of Macbeth to flatter King James as his descendant.

1. Macbeth is their chosen target – **there to meet with Macbeth** – know he is evil
2. Macbeth wants to resist – **why do I yield, unfix my hair**
3. Banquo wants to know – **seeds of time, which grain will grow**
4. Banquo resists acting on knowledge – **instruments of darkness, win us to our harm**
5. Macbeth equivocates – **if good, if ill,**
6. Macbeth can resist on his own, so enlists wife's evil – **letter, jump the life to come**
7. Killing of Banquo leads to divine, supernatural intervention – Banquo's ghost
8. Banquo's ghost, supernatural reveals Macbeth's regicide to the nobles – **never shake they gory locks at me, thou canst not say I did it**
9. Goes back to the witches – **something wicked this way comes** – they are not the wicked ones, just give true prophecies, Macbeth chooses evil actions
10. Prophecies are tricks, he is a willing victim – **juggling fiends no more believed**
11. Nihilistic rejection of God and the supernatural – **life is a tale told by an idiot**
12. Welcomes death – **such a one am I to fear/forgot the taste of fears**
13. Conclusion – noble ancestor Banquo, evil butcher Macbeth, cautionary tale, eternal damnation, no joy in regicide.

Ok, let's see how we can limit this to 6 events and a conclusion.

1. Point 1.
2. The extract fits neatly into points 2 - 5. Point 3 precedes this by a few lines, so we can treat it as the same event – they meet the witches.
3. Point 6.
4. Points 7 and 8 are one event.
5. Point 9.
6. Point 10.
7. Point 11.
8. Point 12.

One solution is to write about Point 1 and 9 at the same time, as they are both the same idea, revealing Macbeth's inherent wickedness. The witches only reveal what is already there. The advantage of that is that you also get to start with the extract!

Point 12 is the easiest one to get rid of, as it is not 100% related to the supernatural.

How Do You Feel?
These plans will all get you at least grade 9.

The reason I've done this is to show you that getting a grade 9 is hard, but not that hard. Even if you personally don't know the play well enough to write a plan like this, you might write one 70% as good, which will probably get you a grade 8, or 60% as good which will give you a grade 7.

It is well worth writing your own plans to these questions. Have a go at writing at least one essay.

Because you are going to be shocked at how easy it is to get grades 6 and 7.

Some of you will be shocked at how easy it is to get grades 8 and 9.

At its simplest:

1. Plan chronologically.
2. Write about 6 events, quoting from each.
3. Write as much as you can, as quickly as you can.
4. Start with a thesis, end with a conclusion.

8 Skills of Essay Writing

You will meet 8 Skills which get you top grades, and we'll look at them in every essay. You've already met them in the table recording what students do at each grade.

1. **Thesis Statement** – set it out in 3 parts and write about Shakespeare's purpose
2. **Explanations** – write as many as you can
3. **Quotes** – 13 to 15 and zoom in on individual words
4. **Named Methods** – name a method every time you use a quote if you can, and include structure as a method
5. **Society/era/patriarchal/Jacobean/contemporary/ historical reference etc** – weave them in like embedded quotes to prove your point
6. **Shakespeare** – keep coming back to Shakespeare's purpose – these are easy to link to his methods
7. **Exploratory,** tentative language: **Could, Might, May, Perhaps, Probably** –to show you are writing an 'exploratory response'.
8. **Conclusion**– link to Shakespeare's purposes again.

Level 1

Simple, explicit comments   1–5 marks Grade 1

Marks	Words	Thesis	Exp.	Quote	Methods	Context	Shake	Exp L	Conc.	Para
3	186	N	3	9	0	0	0	0	N	5
3	99	N	0	0	0	0	0	0	N	3
4	139	N	4	2	0	0	3	0	Y	3
5	312	N	2	3	0	0	1	2	N	3
Ave	184	N	2	4	0	0	1	0	N	3

Key

The essays have a system of underlining, bold and italic to help you see how these skills are used at each grade.

- Thesis statement
- *Explanation words*
- **Quote**
- METHODS
- <u>**Context**</u>
- <u>Shakespeare</u>
- Exploratory language*
- Conclusion

Question 1

Response 1

This extract *reveals* Macbeth's violence to win in battle. Duncan learns about Macbeth's part in the battle from the captain.

The captain says, "**doubtful it stood**". That *shows* Macbeth has "**multiplying villainies of nature.**"

He says that Macbeth "**well deserves**" to change his name, even though he is "**disdaining fortune**". His "**brandished steel**" is being "**smoked with bloody execution like valour's minion**".

Macbeth is "**unseamed**" because he "**ne'er shook hands, but not to make farewell**". This *means* order and disorder. To have "**th'chaps**" *means* that he is masculine. Macbeth wants to become king after his victory. This is what the witches meant by "**foul is fair, fair is foul.**"

After this, Macbeth becomes evil and acts bravely. He becomes king and then needs to assassinate Banquo. Later in the play he seems to be too brave and overconfident.

Original 186 words

3 marks

- **Thesis Statement No**
- **Explanations 3**
- **Quotes 9**
- **Named Methods 0**
- **Society/era/patriarchal/Jacobean/contemporary/ historical reference etc 0**
- **Shakespeare 0**
- **Exploratory Could, Might, May, Perhaps, Probably 0**
- **Conclusion No**
- **Paragraphs 5**
- **Words per paragraph 37**

My Comments

Focusing on the extract means the student has written rubbish about the quotations, because they don't really understand what the words mean. They've quoted a lot, but what they say about each quote is mostly gibberish.

However, if the student had this approach: 'just write down all the examples where we find out that Macbeth is brave and evil', would they know enough about the play to have a list of at least 5 moments in the play?

I think they would have done, and could easily have scored many more marks.

Examiner Comments

- The response mainly focuses only on the extract.
- It uses lots of quotes.
- There are some simple comments.
- The first sentence has some awareness of ideas.
- Although some of the answer just tells the story, it does show some knowledge of the play as a whole.
- The student doesn't have any awareness of the writer.

Question 4

Response 2

Both Banquo and Macbeth are shocked in this extract, and don't truly believe in what the witches have said.

But, in the rest of the play, they both change their view of the supernatural, as they completely believe in the truth of the witches' words.

In fact, Macbeth is so convinced by them that he returns to ask them about the future of his kingship. He believed that his rule would not be threatened, right up until he died.

Original 99 words

3 marks

- **Thesis Statement No**
- **Explanations 0**
- **Quotes 0**
- **Named Methods 0**
- **Society/era/patriarchal/Jacobean/contemporary/ historical reference 0**
- **Shakespeare 0**
- **Exploratory Could, Might, May, Perhaps, Probably 0**
- **Conclusion No**
- **Paragraphs 3**
- **Words per paragraph 33**

My Comments

The student seems to have a good idea of the plot, picking out that Macbeth went back to the witches.

This sounds like an intelligent student who simply can't be bothered to do well.

Examiner Comments

- There are some relevant details.
- There is one event from the rest of the play.
- This is a student who appears to know very little. If only they had just written some more about the extract, they would get higher marks.

Question 2

Response 3

In this extract Shakespeare presents Lady Macbeth as evil. Her character changes. Her evil is *revealed* when she says "**yet who would have thought the old man to have had so much blood in him?**" This *reveals* that she has no sympathy. She is careless and mostly evil.

Lady Macbeth is female and changes during the play. At the beginning, Shakespeare presented her as charming, but she keeps her evil deep inside her. *We can see this* when she says "**Here's the smell of blood still**".

Shakespeare *shows* how she is a character who isn't useful to anyone, especially in this scene.

Original 139 words

4 marks

- **Thesis Statement No**
- **Explanations 4**
- **Quotes 2**
- **Named Methods 0**
- **Society/era/patriarchal/Jacobean/contemporary/ historical reference etc 0**
- **Shakespeare 3**
- **Exploratory Could, Might, May, Perhaps, Probably 0**
- **Conclusion Yes**
- **Paragraphs 3**
- **Words per paragraph 46**

My Comments

As we will see again and again, starting with the extract really gets in the way. It means the student has pretty much only written about the extract.

What if they had written a plan first?

If they had just listed up to 6 events which show she is evil, and then any quotes they could remember about her, this student would have gained so many more marks.

Examiner Comments

- This makes some simple, relevant comments.
- There is one relevant detail.

- The word 'reveals' shows that the student is aware that the writer is making deliberate choices.
- The essay is beginning to be aware of ideas, as we see in the abstract idea of 'evil'.
- The student is general, rather than specific.

Question 4

Response 4

When Macbeth is made Thane of Cawdor, he thinks that **this means** the supernatural is "good". So he says, "**I am Thane of Cawdor. If good, why, do I yield to that suggestion**." He likes this promotion. Maybe* Duncan made Macbeth the Thane of Cawdor to stop Macbeth being lonely, to make him important and superior to others.

<u>Shakespeare</u> **portrays** Banquo and Macbeth having a negative attitude to the supernatural, because the witches prophesised that Macbeth would be Thane of Cawdor.

In the extract, Macbeth says "**knock at my ribs against the use of nature**", which is negative. This might* allude to "**dashed its brains out**", which was the violence towards the baby. So both are violent images.

Original 312 words

5 marks

- **Thesis Statement No**
- **Explanations 2**
- **Quotes 3**
- **Named Methods 0**
- **Society/era/patriarchal/Jacobean/contemporary/ historical reference 0**
- **Shakespeare 1**
- **Exploratory Could, Might, May, Perhaps, Probably 2**
- **Conclusion No**
- **Paragraphs 3**
- **Words per paragraph 104**

My Comments

How difficult would it have been for this student to write down as many examples of the supernatural as they could?

That's how many more points they could have made. For each one it would be easy to find a reference or a quote. Without knowing any more of the play, they could have doubled their marks in the next band.

Examiner Comments

- Most of this is Level 1, with simple comments.

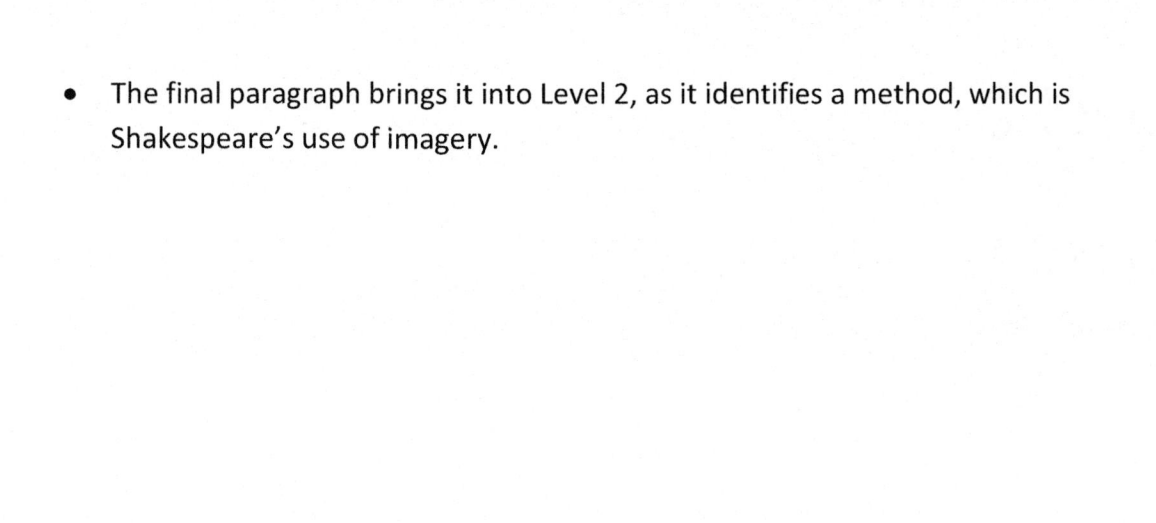

- The final paragraph brings it into Level 2, as it identifies a method, which is Shakespeare's use of imagery.

Level 2

Supported, relevant comments   6–10 marks
Grade 2

Marks	Words	Thesis	Exp.	Quote	Methods	Context	Shake	Exp L	Conc.	Para
7	256	N	5	3	0	1	4	0	N	4

(AQA just don't seem to publish answers at this level – I have no idea why).

Question 2

Response 5

In this extract <u>Shakespeare</u> portrays Lady Macbeth as both open and risk taking. **We can see this** when she says "**Banquo's buried, he cannot come out on's grave**". She is abrupt and direct. She gives detailed information, but her tone is unconcerned.

However, <u>Shakespeare</u> also portrays her guilt, which is *revealed* when she tells Macbeth "**wash your hands, put on your night gown.**" The action "**wash your hands**" *implies* that she is feeling guilt about her part in Banquo's death.

In addition, <u>Shakespeare</u> portrays her as curious, when she says "**yet who would have thought the old man to have had so much blood in him**". *This tells us* that, though she planned the murder, she is surprised how much blood came out of Banquo's corpse.

<u>Shakespeare</u> *presents her* as <u>typical of women in Elizabethan society</u>. She would remain at home, cooking and cleaning for her husband. This is expected of her. But she quickly becomes eager to become queen once Macbeth has become Thane of Cawdor. She manipulates Macbeth to kill Banquo so that they can become king and queen. This is how <u>Shakespeare</u> *shows* that Lady Macbeth changes.

Original 256 words

7 marks

- **Thesis Statement No**
- **Explanations 5**
- **Quotes 3**

- Society/era/patriarchal/Jacobean/contemporary/ historical reference etc 1
- Named Methods 0
- Shakespeare 4
- Exploratory Could, Might, May, Perhaps, Probably 0
- Conclusion No
- Paragraphs 4
- Words per paragraph 64

My Comments

Writing about a character is the easiest question to plan. You simply write down what you know about the character, in chronological order.

Then next to each fact or event, you write any quotes you know.

It is impossible that this student didn't know "unsex me here", "dashed it's brains out", "coward", "cruelty", and so on.

It is impossible that this student didn't know Lady Macbeth persuaded Macbeth to kill Duncan, that she had to tell him to take the daggers back…

Under exam conditions, the student has decided the king was called Banquo. This probably wouldn't have happened with a 6 point plan.

All of these would have been easy to write about if only the student had written a chronological plan and not started with the extract!

Examiner Comments

- The opening makes an implicit comment about the writer's methods.
- Relevant comments about references to the play happen throughout the essay.
- The weakest element is AO2, where the student doesn't have enough examples of portray or presents, or other words showing that they are looking at what the writer is doing.

Level 3

Explained, structured comments   11–15 marks
Grade 3 - 4

Marks	Words	Thesis	Exp.	Quote	Methods	Context	Shake	Exp L	Conc.	Para
12	838	N	15	8	3	3	3	1	Y	7
13	416	N	10	2	0	1	4	0	Y	5
14	308	Y	8	3	1	2	2	1	N	4
Ave	521	N	11	4	1	2	3	1	Y	5

Question 2

Response 6

In this extract, <u>Shakespeare</u> presents Lady Macbeth as sleep walking, and revealing things no one else should know. She says, "**Here's the smell of blood still: all the perfumes of Arabia will not sweeten this little hand.**" *This means* that no amount of perfume can take away the smell of blood which is on her hands. The phrase "**Here's the smell of blood**" *proves* that she is a murderer, and that her hands still smell of the victim's blood. This is a disease which makes <u>a contemporary audience</u> sympathise with her, even though she has done something bad.

<u>Shakespeare</u> *portrays* her as a sick woman with mental issues, which cause her to reveal details she should not reveal, while she sleep walks. The quote "**what's done is done, cannot be undone**" *proves* she can't go back in time and undo what she has done. So, she must've done something bad, and now she feels guilty, and wants not to have done it, but she can't go back. The verb "**done**" *tells us* she had probably* done something. She can't do anything about what "**cannot be undone**". She did a bad thing. She killed King Duncan. We feel sorry for her as she feels guilty and wishes she hadn't done this bad thing.

She says things which she shouldn't say. Shakespeare presents her as saying "**wash your hands ... he cannot come out on's grave**". *This tells* us she is talking to Macbeth, telling him to wash his hands after killing Banquo. She tells him to look pale, because Banquo cannot come back to life and come out of his grave. She is commanding Macbeth "**wash your hands**", which *suggests* she controls him. It also *shows* that Macbeth has killed Banquo, so now his hands are bloody, and he needs to wash them.

At the start, Lady Macbeth was powerful, and controlled Macbeth. This quote *proves* it: "**look like the innocent flower, but be the serpent under't**". The **SIMILE** *means* she wants Macbeth to appear good and kind to King Duncan, but as soon as the time is right, to kill him. The **METAPHOR** "**But be the serpent under't**" *shows* that Lady Macbeth and Macbeth are planning to murder Duncan at the right time. The Jacobean audience would be so sad for Duncan, as he believes the Macbeths are loyal to him, but instead they have planned to murder him. Women were powerless in the Jacobean era, and were always controlled by men. But Lady Macbeth is strong and powerful. She controls Macbeth.

In the middle of the play, Lady Macbeth is brave. She is malevolent. She asks spirits, "**come you spirits, unsex me here**". *This means* she wants them to remove her femininity and fill her up with cruelty. She wants to change gender, which is *revealed* in the verb "**unsex**". She wants this so she has the ability to murder kind Duncan. This command also *implies* that she is brave, because she is controlling spirits. Jacobean women were supposed to be weak and controlled by men, but not Lady Macbeth, who is powerful and controls her husband.

At the end of the play, she has a disease, which is sleep walking. *We know this* from the doctor. He says. "**This disease is beyond my practice**". He also says "**I have known those which have walked in their sleep who have died holily in their beds.**" This *implies* those who sleep walk will die. This **FORESHADOWS** that Lady Macbeth will die.

At the start, Lady Macbeth was powerful. In the middle, she wanted to be stronger and asked for the help of spirits. At the end she becomes so weak and powerless. She will die because she has the disease of sleep walking.

Original 838 words

12 marks

- **Thesis Statement No**
- **Explanations 15**
- **Quotes 8**
- **Named Methods 3**
- **Society/era/patriarchal/Jacobean/contemporary/ historical reference etc 3**
- **Shakespeare 3**
- **Exploratory Could, Might, May, Perhaps, Probably 1**

- **Conclusion** Yes
- **Paragraphs** 7
- **Words per paragraph** 120

My Comments

Writing about the extract is what this student does least well. They jump into analysing quotes they don't understand. She didn't kill Duncan. Macbeth didn't have actual blood on his hands after having Banquo killed. Sleepwalking is probably not a disease!

However, the student has learned the quotes they want to write about from elsewhere in the play.

The essay gets much better when they write about those, and move through the play in chronological order.

Because they started with the extract, there is a lot of waffle. Luckily, this student was able to write over 800 words, so they still had time to hoover up marks by writing about the rest of the play.

But imagine the marks they could have got if they started with a thesis about why Shakespeare wanted to present Lady Macbeth in these ways. The student would then have written much more about Shakespeare's purpose, and each 'way' would count as a method.

You should also notice, as we move up the mark scheme, that abstract ideas prove you are more 'thoughtful' or 'convincing'. These ideas include **ambition, guilt, psychology, manipulation, hamartia, etc** and **the contemporary ideas of 1605, The Great Chain of Being** and **The Divine Right of Kings.**

Examiner Comments

- The essay starts with some comments about the extract, backed up by references.
- The essay starts to deal with ideas with the abstract word 'guilt'.
- The student works through the play chronologically, which is really helpful, as it allows them to make lots of appropriate references.
- By the end, they have explained ideas about the whole task.
- There are not enough references to methods or Shakespeare's ideas.

Question 1

Response 7

We can see Macbeth's bravery as a soldier with the words "**For brave Macbeth – well he deserves that name**." Shakespeare *presents* him as a national hero. We can see this as the captain is proud of Macbeth's heroism. This also *reveals* Macbeth's loyalty to Duncan and Scotland.

The battle *portrays* Macbeth as relentless in order to win, "**till he unseamed him from the nave to th'chaps**". This *suggests* his violence is endless. However, because this serves king and country, this violence is heroic. The captain's praise of Macbeth *presents* him as the most significant warrior in the battle.

Shakespeare *portrays* Macbeth as influenced by Lady Macbeth, in deciding to murder Duncan. Macbeth's ambition allowed him to use his violent nature to commit this violent act, without worrying about it.

Shakespeare *suggests* that **we all have a fatal flaw**, like Macbeth. His ambition was his **fatal flaw**. He planned to kill Duncan and steal the title of king. This also *portrays* Macbeth as a criminal. He turns to crime in order to satisfy his ambition. We can see that he is ruthless because he had been loyal to Duncan. This *reveals* how the power of greed can affect anyone's actions.

In conclusion, in the extract Shakespeare *suggests* Macbeth's violence was necessary. He used it for a good cause. He also seems more bloodthirsty in the extract than when he murdered Duncan. This *suggests* that he chose to murder Duncan quickly in order to satisfy his own greed, rather than the violence of battle which was gory because it was for an honourable cause.

Original 416 words

13 marks

- **Thesis Statement No**
- **Explanations 10**
- **Quotes 2**
- **Named Methods 0**
- **Society/era/patriarchal/Jacobean/contemporary/ historical reference etc 1**
- **Shakespeare 4**
- **Exploratory Could, Might, May, Perhaps, Probably 0**
- **Conclusion Yes**

- **Paragraphs 5**
- **Words per paragraph 83**

My Comments

The answer is 'limited' because it deals with only one other incident in the play, the murder of Duncan.

Sure, the student gains extra marks because they are able to write about language by starting with the extract. But do you believe the student knew no other times when Macbeth was violent, and no other violent quotes – nothing about 'blood' for instance, or scorching snakes, or scorpions.

I think the student could have spent 2 minutes writing a list of evidence of Macbeth's violence, and any quotes they could remember. Then they could have written a much fuller answer.

Once again, focusing on the extract has stopped the student getting the mark they deserve.

The other thing you will notice is effort. This student is much more academic than the one writing response 6. They got one more mark in half the words. So, what if this student had decided to write 800 words? They would easily have scored 20 marks.

Words, words, words. Make your writing speed a priority.

Examiner Comments

- The student sometimes explains and uses references.
- Comments are supported by references in the first two paragraphs.
- The focus on fatal flaw and loyalty is level 3.
- By the end, the essay is a good explanation.
- It focuses very little on the writer's methods.

Question 2

Response 8

Shakespeare portrays Lady Macbeth as both consumed by guilt and changing as the play develops.

This is evident when she instructs "**out damned spot!**" where she wants to remove all traces of blood from her hand. This is the first time her guilt is *revealed*, and *illustrates* how she now begins to regret the immorality of her actions. The **IMPERATIVE** "**out**" *illustrates* her sense of urgency in removing the blood.

Throughout the play, Shakespeare *presents* her as controlling Macbeth, manipulating him toward immorality. *We see this* when she commands "**unsex me here**". She wishes to become less of a woman, with a man's power, rather than a man's sex. However, this forceful tone and desire for male power is later replaced with emotions of guilt and disgust at her own actions.

We also see her character change in other ways. She was desperate to kill Duncan, only to find that, because he looked like her father, she couldn't carry out the murder, leaving it instead to Macbeth. We know a **Jacobean audience** would have been horrified at Lady Macbeth's actions. They would be disturbed by her control of Macbeth and how she pushes him towards evil acts, as this also *portrays* him as weak. Some *might* view* the way her character changes as evidence that **she is a witch**.

Original 308 words

14 marks

- **Thesis Statement Yes**
- **Explanations 8**
- **Quotes 3**
- **Named Methods 1**
- **Society/era/patriarchal/Jacobean/contemporary/ historical reference etc 2**
- **Shakespeare 2**
- **Exploratory Could, Might, May, Perhaps, Probably 1**
- **Conclusion No**
- **Paragraphs 4**
- **Words per paragraph 77**

My Comments

Well, everything I wrote about Response 7 counts here! This is an even more academic student, who has smashed out 300 words and then chilled.

Write as though you are being pursued by a T-Rex which feeds on ink and blood – feed it ink instead.

Although they realise a thesis statement is helpful – it reminded them to write about the rest of the play – they forgot the main point of a thesis. It is to set out 3 ideas about Shakespeare's purpose. This immediately makes your essay at least 'thoughtful' and will mean that you always end up writing about 'methods' and the writer's 'perspective'.

Examiner Comments

- The essay has a clear focus on the abstract idea of guilt from the start, and then there are many more in the essay.
- There are many relevant references.
- The student should write about more methods.

Level 4

Clear understanding

16–20 marks Grades 5 and 6

Marks	Words	Thesis	Exp.	Quote	Methods	Context	Shake	Exp L	Conc.	Para
16	488	Y	9	8	1	1	1	0	N	7
16	584	N	9	8	2	2	2	2	N	5
18	779	Y	16	11	6	3	1	0	Y	10
18	710	Y	9	8	1	7	1	3	Y	7
19	355	Y	9	9	2	4	0	0	Y	6
Ave	583	Y	10	10	2	3	1	1	Y	7

Question 1

Response 9

Macbeth can be both celebrated and criticised for his violence, which we see in this extract and in the rest of the play.

This extract describes Macbeth's violence in battle. **This is** praiseworthy as he is defending his country. The captain describes him as "**brave**" and he respects the fact that he killed many soldiers. **This is typical** of how others would view Macbeth.

Macbeth also chooses to act very violently in battle. He "**unseamed**" his enemy "**from the nave to th'chaps and fixed his head upon our battlements**". This *implies* Macbeth has always had a violent character, before he hears the witches' prophecies.

Macbeth is also violent elsewhere in the play, which we see when he murders Duncan. We *understand* Macbeth has violent thoughts when he speaks in **SOLILOQUY**. These thoughts

43

are so strong that, as he prepares to kill Duncan, his mind creates a vision, "**is this a dagger I see before me**"? Macbeth has an emotionless reaction to murdering Duncan, saying "**It is done**". This *suggests* that he is so violent in nature that he has no sympathy or guilt.

In the extract, Shakespeare *shows* that Macbeth's sword "**smoked with bloody execution**". This *reveals* that Macbeth's violence has led him to kill so many soldiers that his sword is dripping in death and slaughter.

We *understand* that killing has become normal for him, and accepted by his society. This is why he is called "**valiant cousin**" and a "**worthy gentleman**".

We finally meet Macbeth telling Seyton that he wants to behave violently "**until Birnam Wood moves to Dunsinane**". This *suggests* he will keep fighting until the impossible happens, because he cannot imagine how the wood can ever climb the hill. He believes he cannot be overthrown, so can continue to rule violently.

Original 488 words

16 marks

- **Thesis Statement Yes**
- **Explanations 9**
- **Quotes 8**
- **Named Methods 1**
- **Society/era/patriarchal/Jacobean/contemporary/ historical reference etc 1**
- **Shakespeare 1**
- **Exploratory Could, Might, May, Perhaps, Probably 0**
- **Conclusion No**
- **Paragraphs 7**
- **Words per paragraph 70**

My Comments

You can see that the extract is acting as an anchor. In psychology, an anchor is the idea you are first presented with, which then acts as a weight, drawing you back to it.

For example, if I show you a pair of designer trainers that cost £1000, and then a pair that costs £200, you will think that the £200 pair is cheap. You will probably think that even if you have never spent more than £80 on a pair of trainers before. This is the impact of anchoring.

Here, the anchor is the extract. You can see the student trying to write about events other than the murder of Duncan. This really impresses the examiner, because they are used to reading the weak and poorly constructed answers we have just met. Possibly 50% of students write answers like those.

Whereas, if the student had simply written a list of all the ways that Macbeth is violent, they would have come up with many more ideas.

- The killing of Banquo?
- The slaughter of Macduff's family?
- The fight with Macduff?

Even without remembering any quotes, the sleepiest of students would probably remember these events occurred in the play. Notice that they are also in chronological order.

My comments about the thesis from Response 8 also apply here.

Examiner Comments

- This is a good example of an explained answer.
- The answer focuses on the whole task, with relevant examples from different parts of the play.
- The comments are always relevant to the task.
- There are several comments on the effects of language. For example on the sword which smoked with bloody execution.
- The essay as a whole is consistent enough to get into the bottom of level 4.
- The student could be a bit more explicit about ideas, especially violence.

Question 3

Response 10

Shakespeare *portrays* the relationship of Macbeth and Lady Macbeth as poisonous and manipulative in this extract. Here Macbeth complains, and she replies "**What do you mean?**" She challenges him, and does not treat him as having a higher status. *This demonstrates* her ambition and control, because contemporary women were treated as inferior to men. Lady Macbeth commands Macbeth with **IMPERATIVES**: "**go**", "**give**", "**bring**" and "**carry**". He obeys and she continues to give him instructions throughout the play.

In public they *appear* different, with Macbeth as a noble warrior and Lady Macbeth as a powerless female. However, in their communication with each other, she is clearly most powerful. Macbeth is all over the place and desperate for affection when he tells his wife, "**I am afraid to think what I have done**". She ridicules him, making him feel powerless, replying "**Infirm of purpose**". This short sentence might* also *suggest* that she has no love for him, and instead simply uses her husband in order to achieve power.

She commands him to "**Give me the daggers**". She *shows* she is more powerful than him, as she gets on with his job, because he is unable to do it. Jacobean women were believed to be too weak to perform such tasks, which *emphasises* that Lady Macbeth has become more powerful than her husband. However, this changes later in the play. At one point she tries to boss Macbeth, and instead of business as usual, he replies "**Hold they tongue**", by which he means 'shut up'. This *implies* that perhaps* he only allows her a sense of power when it suits him.

At other times Lady Macbeth nurtures Macbeth. For example, when he sees Banquo's ghost, she tells all the guests to leave, because he is "**sick**". She cares for him and asks what is troubling him. This *implies* respect and love for each other.

Shakespeare also uses the **MOTIF** of sleep in this extract and later in the play. Sleep *reveals* their relationship is a struggle for power. It begins with Macbeth being unable to sleep, and then Lady Macbeth gradually goes mental because she is unable to sleep.

Original 584 words

16 marks

- **Thesis Statement No**
- **Explanations 9**
- **Quotes 8**
- **Named Methods 2**

- **Society/era/patriarchal/Jacobean/contemporary/ historical reference etc 2**
- **Shakespeare 2**
- **Exploratory Could, Might, May, Perhaps, Probably 2**
- **Conclusion No**
- **Paragraphs 5**
- **Words per paragraph 117**

My Comments

I really like the examiner's comments below.

The easiest way for this student to get higher marks would have been to write that thesis statement, with three of Shakespeare's ideas or reasons for presenting Lady Macbeth in these ways.

If they had worked through the play chronologically they would also have written a better argument. Without that, the last two paragraphs appear as afterthoughts.

Examiner Comments

- The first paragraph shows that the student has a clear understanding of the task.
- They use details and context to write about the controlling relationship. But the context is a bit too general to get into Level 4 for AO3.
- Lady Macbeth's language is analysed well in the opening paragraphs. But the language analysis isn't strongly linked to Shakespeare's ideas.
- For example, there is no clear reason why the short sentence shows that she doesn't love Macbeth.
- The answer is detailed enough to be judged as sustained.
- To improve the student needs to link Shakespeare's methods to his ideas.

Question 2

Response 11

Shakespeare presents Lady Macbeth as elegant and sophisticated at the beginning of the play. However, as the play develops, she is revealed as a villain, manipulative and **Machiavellian**.

For example, in Act 5 Scene 1, Lady Macbeth is trapped in her visions while sleepwalking. She tells herself to "**wash your hands**", which *displays* her guilt at having manipulated Macbeth to murder both Duncan and Banquo. She believed in the witches' prophecies, that she and Macbeth would have ultimate power as king and queen.

Her evil nature is most clearly *demonstrated* in Act 2 and Act 3. Here she tells Macbeth to "**Be the innocent flower**". This **METAPHOR** *reveals* that she has no fear of inflicting psychological pain on Macbeth, and of brainwashing him. Her selfish nature is **CONTRASTED** with the way he worships her, and *we see* her selfishness throughout the play.

In this extract, Lady Macbeth is like a spoilt brat. She suffers from guilt because of the evil acts she has commanded Macbeth to commit out of love for her. However, while sleepwalking she also tries to rid herself of her guilt. She repeats "**to bed, to bed**", *emphasising* her female nature, which tries to *suggest* her innocence. She *appears* **typically female** by being caring and loving, telling Macbeth "**put on your nightgown, look not so pale. I tell you again, Banquo's buried; he cannot come out on's grave**". *But in reality*, she is evil and manipulative, plotting the death of others for her own gain.

We see her power over Macbeth when she takes over the planning of Duncan's murder. This is uncommon in a **Jacobean woman**. In **CONTRAST** to his wife's excitement at becoming a powerful and wealthy queen, Macbeth's mind is filled with "**scorpions**". This is a **METAPHOR**. The noun "**scorpions**" *shows* how guilty Macbeth feels in **CONTRAST** to his wife's happiness.

Furthermore, in this extract, Lady Macbeths imagines she can sense "**the smell of blood still**". This hallucination *reveals* the ghosts of Duncan and Banquo are getting karmic revenge on her for persuading Macbeth to murder them. To sum up, Lady Macbeth *appears* to be more masculine than her husband, even though he actually commits the murders. She belittled him, accusing him of being a "**coward**" and told him to be a "**man**" for her, and this persuaded him to kill.

Late in the extract, she shouts out "**what's done cannot be undone**", which *reveals* how she's become slightly insane because her guilty conscience overwhelms her. However, she tries to minimise her guilt by telling herself that it "**cannot be undone**". In addition, at the start of the play Lady Macbeth took risks: she just desired becoming queen. So she was able to dominate everyone. But, in this extract, *she exhibits* some remorse, so she repeats "**No more o' that**". *We can see* that she feels too overwhelmed by her guilt, so she insists to have "**no more**".

Moreover, even the Doctor doesn't believe he can prevent guilt invading her mind, because she has promoted so much sin. So he says, "**This disease is beyond my practise**". Calling her guilt a "**disease**" which is "**beyond**" his experience *shows* that he can't cure her of sleep-walking. She is going to be dressed in clothes of guilt.

In addition, she insisted "**unsex me here**" to help her manipulate and screw Macbeth about his masculinity. The adverb "**unsex**" *reveals* how she wants to change gender. Consequently, she will kill Duncan for her husband. She has evil ideas and schemes. Furthermore, she wants Macbeth to feel weak, calling him a "**man**" but belittling him for not having the stomach to kill Duncan. She *shows* how disappointed she is in him, and his sense of shame forces him to give his scheming and devious wife what she wants by making her queen.

In conclusion, Macbeth wanted to prove his bloodthirsty wife wrong about his masculinity. Lady Macbeth and Macbeth reveal the two main **THEMES** of the play, guilt and ambition.

Original 779 words

18 marks

- **Thesis Statement Yes**
- **Explanations 16**
- **Quotes 11**
- **Named Methods 6**
- **Society/era/patriarchal/Jacobean/contemporary/ historical reference etc 3**
- **Shakespeare 1**
- **Exploratory Could, Might, May, Perhaps, Probably 0**
- **Conclusion Yes**
- **Paragraphs 10**
- **Words per paragraph 78**

My Comments

I feel for this student. They've written loads. There are 11 quotations. They obviously know the play really well. They should be getting fantastic marks.

However, they write about Lady Macbeth as though she was a real person, rather than a character constructed in order for Shakespeare to play with his ideas and his audience. Examiners call this the need to treat a character as a 'construct'.

It is much easier to explore how the character is constructed if we follow them from beginning to end – how they change and why they change then become 'methods'.

If you don't do that, your essay is likely to be:

- This is what I find out about the character in the extract
- She is also like this in another part of the play.
- Oh, here is another way she behaves in a different part of the play.
- And that reminds me of the extract again – look.
- Oh, and once she behaved like this.
- So, overall, that's what she's like.

Examiner Comments

- The student shows that they know the full chronology of the play right at the start.
- The opening paragraphs shows that they are going to deal with the play as a whole.
- The student links quotes from the extract to quotes from elsewhere in the play.
- AO3 context comments begin as vague ideas, but then get much clearer, so the answer reaches Level 4.
- The student doesn't consider methods enough. Writing about parts of speech is not generally appropriate as these are rarely methods.

Question 3

Response 12

Shakespeare *portrays* the relationship between Macbeth and Lady Macbeth as unusual for the Jacobean era. Jacobeans would expect Macbeth to be dominant, but in this play Lady Macbeth is the dominant one.

In this extract she commands him to "**Go carry them [the daggers] and smear the sleepy grooms**" with blood. She's bossy, pulling his strings, telling him what to do, and *proves* she is the dominant person in the household. She's angry with him for not leaving the daggers by the grooms, instructing him "**They must lie there**". This **IMPERATIVE** "**must**" *reveals* that she understands the plan fully and is really confident. Despite this irritation, she is cool and calm. This is unusual, as she is taking the lead in Duncan's murder, so Shakespeare *presents* the relationship as surprising to a Jacobean audience.

In Act 1 Macbeth tells her that he has changed his mind about killing Duncan. She is disgusted and manipulates him, saying that he will no longer be manly if he doesn't murder Duncan: "**when you durst do it, then you were a man**". So he murders Duncan. A typical wife would probably* try to persuade her husband not to commit murder, so this is strange. But Macbeth wants to prove his manhood to his wife. This isn't normal. Especially in Jacobean times, as there would be consequences if a woman spoke to her husband this way. They have a strange dynamic, because it's *as though* Lady Macbeth is the decision maker and Macbeth is just instructed by her.

At the start they called each other "**partner in greatness**". This *implies* they view each other as equal, even though Lady Macbeth behaves as more powerful, giving Macbeth orders about the murder. Usually the man would be more powerful so this is a strange relationship.

Later, while Lady Macbeth becomes increasingly mad, Macbeth tells her not to worry about his plans to kill Banquo, calling her "**dearest chuck**". Although it *appears* affectionate, compared to "**partner in greatness**" it is demeaning. This patronising dismissal *reveals* that he no longer trusts her and views her as inferior. After everything she's done to help him become king, Macbeth should trust her. She is a queen. So this is an unusual dynamic.

Back to the extract, Macbeth tells her he "**dare not**" go in to see Duncan's dead body because he is "**afraid**" to see what he has done. Lady Macbeth goes in instead, saying "**Give me the daggers**". This is surprising as Macbeth is probably* the best warrior in Scotland. Only that morning he had "**unseamed**" an enemy who was his friend, but now Macbeth is strangely afraid, and his wife is having to do his job for him. It's inconceivable. A gorgeous wife is braver than her noble warrior husband. Weird. Shakespeare *portrays* their

51

relationship as exceptionally odd, and would **shock a Jacobean audience**, because a warrior should be better at this than a woman. To them it is unbelievable. And that's how the relationship is presented as weird.

In conclusion, their relationship is presented as unusual in order to shock **the contemporary audience** with the concept that a woman could be more powerful than her husband during this era.

Original 710 words

18 marks

- Thesis Statement Yes
- Explanations 9
- Quotes 8
- Named Methods 1
- Society/era/patriarchal/Jacobean/contemporary/ historical reference etc 7
- Shakespeare 1
- Exploratory Could, Might, May, Perhaps, Probably 2
- Conclusion Yes
- Paragraphs 7
- Words per paragraph 100

My Comments

Everything I wrote about Response 11 is true here.

You've probably noticed, throughout the answers so far, that students have a strange mix of formal and informal vocabulary.

When I rewrite the students' answers, I use exactly the same quotes, arguments and sentence structures.

I have to change the vocabulary so that it isn't plagiarism. But, I try to keep exactly the same levels of formality. For example, the one word sentence "Weird" in the original was a one word sentence "Strange".

Although there aren't direct marks for how well you express yourself, there is one dramatic way this will improve your grade. This answer is actually 531 words long, compared to the actual answer which was 710 words. That's a 25% reduction.

I could have reduced it by a lot more, and still got exactly the same marks, but then you would lose the informal tone.

But, the point is this: the more formal you are, the less waffle you will use. This means you have time in the exam to write 25% more! That will get you a lot more marks, and a higher grade.

So, a good way to practise is to take an answer like this and rewrite it to get more marks.

Examiner Comments

- This is typical of students who make generalised comments about context and gender. We see this at the beginning. It gets some marks, though, because it references Shakespearian society.
- The context is better explained later when writing about trust and equality, which is Level 4 AO3.
- There are lots of comments supported by references to the text.
- The student selects a range of appropriate moments from the rest of the play to back up their ideas. There are enough of these to be sustained for Level 4 AO1.
- The student should focus more on methods.

Question 1

Response 13

This **"tale of sound and fury"** *reveals* Macbeth's tragedy. <u>**Disrupting the Great Chain of Being**</u> and challenging <u>**divine rule**</u> leads to a cycle of violence.

The captain describes Macbeth as **"brave Macbeth"** in his **"bloody execution"** of Macdonald. Macbeth is seen as superior because he has managed to kill a Thane. The phrase **"bloody execution"** *reveals* his ruthlessness and his violent nature. **"Bloody"** FORESHADOWS how Macbeth will be drawn towards committing evil acts.

Macbeth killed Macdonald and then **"fixed his head upon our battlements"**. This public display *suggests* that he enjoys violence. To Duncan and his nobles this is seen as heroic. However, his actions appear boastful. This *suggests* he uses violence in order to hide his insecurities.

We come to loathe Macbeth as we meet his later actions. He begins as valiant and noble character, but ends as a paranoid coward. He imagines himself caught **"in blood"** once he has murdered Duncan. *We realise* he feels so much guilt that he will never feel at peace, when he tells us **"the Thane of Cawdor and Glamis should sleep no more"**.

Being caught **"in blood"** also *implies* that he will always be corrupt, and his character is permanently damaged. This is why the witches say something **"wicked"** is coming towards them as Macbeth comes to see them. They are a supernatural influence and <u>**disturb the natural order**</u>. *This means* that their words are IRONIC. The witches are known to be evil and inhuman, yet they see Macbeth as particularly **"wicked"**. This *portrays* him as destructive.

Macbeth's ambition is his <u>**hamartia**</u>, and this leads him towards violence, which inevitably ends in his death.

Original 355 words

19 marks

- Thesis Statement Yes
- Explanations 9
- Quotes 9
- Named Methods 2
- Society/era/patriarchal/Jacobean/contemporary/ historical reference etc 4
- Shakespeare 0
- Exploratory Could, Might, May, Perhaps, Probably 0

- **Conclusion Yes**
- **Paragraphs 6**
- **Words per paragraph 60**

My Comments

This was half the length of response 12! This is what I mean by the advantage of using academic language.

Notice how this student has been able to find more quotations from other parts of the text.

I believe this was easier for them because they had already planned their first quote – they were going to use this, no matter what the question.

This allowed them to make a strong start. Crucially, it meant that they were not anchored to the extract, so would later be able to use quotes from different parts of the text.

These, like Macbeth as "wicked" can easily be linked to any key word in the question. It fits violence, but also kingship, the supernatural, Macbeth as a tragic hero, and so on. You can easily pick on single word or two word quotes like this to help with any essay:

"Butcher, wicked, fiend-like, hell-kite, deep damnation, scorpions, serpent, snake, unsex me, murdering ministers, pretty chickens, dagger, damned spot, brief candle…" etc, etc.

It is also really easy to prepare what you want to say about these so that it includes 'methods'. For example, ***'snake' and 'serpent' involve a Christian allusion to Original Sin.*** (The one committed by Adam and Eve).

The animal imagery – these and 'scorpions' and 'kite' – all reveal how Macbeth has lost his status in the eyes of God after his attack on The Great Chain of Being.

The preoccupation with 'hell' and 'damnation' emphasises the Christian message of the play as a cautionary tale.

Everything above in bold would fit *every* essay. Those methods are money in the bank. Look how frequently the examiner keeps advising students to deal with more methods, and to write meaningfully about context.

You could find a lot more one and two word quotes from the notes you already have on the play from school.

Of course, if you know you want to use these methods and quotes from the start, you know the best way to make sure you use them:

Write a chronological plan!

But, look how short this answer is. Sure, this student is highly skilled. But soooo lazy. What would they score if they wrote 800 words?

Examiner Comments

- This is a clear and consistent answer.
- Ideas are clearly explained with effective references to back up the explanations.
- It is Level 4 AO1 references by the time the essay deals with the quote "fixed his head".
- The essay deals with abstract ideas, like guilt and reputation. These are Level 4 for AO3 and AO1.
- The essay needs more analysis of writer's methods. The only real example is the analysis of the word 'bloody'. As it stands, AO2 is therefore Level 3.

Level 5

Thoughtful, developed consideration 21–25 marks Grades 7 and 8

Marks	Words	Thesis	Exp.	Quote	Methods	Context	Shake	Exp L	Conc.	Para
22	763	Y	20	8	5	5	7	2	Y	6
22	561	N	12	5	3	5	3	4	Y	5
24	861	Y	19	13	3	4	1	1	Y	9
25	855	Y	22	11	4	9	5	3	Y	8
Ave	760	Y	18	9	4	6	4	3	Y	7

Question 3

Response 14

Shakespeare *portrays* the relationship between Lady Macbeth and Macbeth as passionate. They start the play as equals. Then throughout the play he uses **IMPERATIVE** verbs and structural devices to show how they manipulate each other. In this extract Shakespeare repeats **IMPERATIVE** verbs to *portray* Lady Macbeth controlling Macbeth. She commands Macbeth to "**go**" to fetch water, and to "**go**" with the daggers. This **REPETITION** *reveals* that she has significant control over her husband.

However, this introduces conflict in their relationship. He refuses her domineering instructions, saying he will "**go no more**". Her command of Macbeth would have **shocked Jacobean audiences**, as women were expected to be submissive and were judged as inferior. However, Lady Macbeth subverts these **gender roles**, and Shakespeare *presents* her as having most power in the relationship. She is also *presented* as powerful when Shakespeare *shows* her manipulating Macbeth. She asks "**why**" he "**unbend**"s his "**noble strength**" after committing **regicide**. This questioning undermines him. Answering "**why**" forces him to question and doubt himself. Calling his strength "**noble**" allows her to

57

manipulate him, making Macbeth want to satisfy her. She uses language skilfully to control him.

She also questions his masculinity when persuading him to murder Duncan. She challenges him to prove if he is a "**man**" rather than appear to be a "**coward**" in her eyes. This *emphasises* both her level of power, and how highly Macbeth values her judgement of him. In this extract, <u>Shakespeare</u> *portrays* Macbeth as reliant on his wife. He depends on her cunning use of language to motivate him to kill Duncan. After killing, Macbeth is astonished to find that he is "**afraid to think what**" he has "**done**" in committing <u>regicide</u>. He confesses this to her, which *reveals* that he trusts her, as well as relying on her to reassure him. Being "**afraid**" *implies* that he may* actually fear his own character. But voicing these fears *reveals* that he relies on Lady Macbeth. *We see this* when he writes to her as "**partner of greatness**" in Act 1. This phrase causes her to feel she is his equal.

However, he writes to her in **<u>PROSE rather than in IAMBIC PENTAMETER</u>**. This challenges our perceptions that the relationship is between equals. <u>Shakespeare **used iambic pentameter when characters of high status speak to each other**</u>. **Prose was used when speaking to the lower classes.** Although the noun "**partner**" *suggests* they are equal, the letter itself is in prose, which contradicts this through the structure of his language. The letter is therefore how Macbeth manipulates his wife into plotting the assassination of Duncan. This *reveals* his power in the relationship. He is **<u>conforming to Jacobean society's expectations</u>** to hold power over a woman.

<u>Shakespeare</u> gives Macbeth a cold **TONE** to reveal his lack of love for Lady Macbeth. When he hears that she has died, he observes "**she should have died hereafter**" which *appears* indifferent. His coldness *implies* that his ambition for power has prevented him loving Lady Macbeth. He *appears** to be saying she would "**have died**" anyway, without committing suicide. This *suggests* his ambition has been so great that it has led to tyrannical rule over Scotland and a destruction of affection, passion and love for Lady Macbeth.

In conclusion, <u>Shakespeare</u> *portrays* the relationship as controlling. He uses language and structure *to show* both spouses manipulate each other and seek to dominate, which leads to their loveless marriage and finally to their deaths.

Original 763 words

22 marks

- **Thesis Statement Yes**
- **Explanations 20**
- **Quotes 8**
- **Named Methods 5**
- **Society/era/patriarchal/Jacobean/contemporary/ historical reference etc 5**

- **Shakespeare 7**
- **Exploratory Could, Might, May, Perhaps, Probably 2**
- **Conclusion Yes**
- **Paragraphs 6**
- **Words per paragraph 127**

My Comments

You'll notice that at this level students have a better vocabulary for writing about literature: tone, prose, iambic pentameter, manipulate, gender roles, submissive, inferior, domineering, imperative…

So a good way to revise is to write down the words which impress you. Put the essay aside, and try to write your own sentences using those words to explain any quotation.

This is the first essay with a proper thesis statement, focusing on Shakespeare's purpose. However, adding why he wants to portray them both as manipulating would have made this an even better thesis.

Notice how writing about the letter, and the language of power, has really impressed the examiner.

Other students don't write about the letter in this question, which is strange. Knowing about the purpose of prose and iambic pentameter is not a difficult piece of knowledge. Any student can learn it. Why don't they mention it then?

Well, mainly it is because they start with the extract.

If you work through the question chronologically, the letter will be relevant to 100% of essays about Lady Macbeth, or the marriage, and probably about 70% of the questions on Macbeth himself.

Examiner Comments

- The answer starts by identifying methods, and showing some awareness of abstract ideas like 'control' and 'gender'.
- AO3 is developed strongly when the essay deals with the power relationships between Lady Macbeth and her husband.
- The discussion about the play as a whole, and the later events of the play makes this a thoughtful and detailed response.
- The part examining Macbeth's reaction to her death is particularly strong.
- To get in to Level 6, the student should link the AO2 language analysis to Shakespeare's ideas with more detail.

Question 4

Response 15

In this extract Macbeth is sceptical of the witches' prophecies. He knows he should be cautious, as they are "**instruments of darkness**". However, the witches used "**supernatural soliciting**" and planted his ambition and his desire to know further prophecies.

In **CONTRAST**, Shakespeare *presents* Banquo as not tempted by the witches. He recognises that they are both deceitful and wicked, and should therefore be resisted. He describes them as "**instruments of darkness**". This acts **SYMBOLICALLY**. "**Darkness**" *represents* the horrors of evil. Banquo *implies* the witches are **tools of Satan**, used to manipulate people towards evil by deceiving them. This is why he cautions Macbeth that the supernatural try to "**win us with honest trifles to betrays in deepest consequences**". Perhaps* Banquo is certain the prophecies are a supernatural trap for Macbeth. *He might* believe* that the witches will manipulate Macbeth so that he too becomes deceitful, and he might* foresee Macbeth's tragedy.

We can see that Macbeth can't resist them, and is curious: "**this supernatural soliciting cannot be ill, cannot be good. If ill, why hath it given earnest of success**". Here he questions whether the prophecies are good or evil. He knows the witches are untrustworthy, just as **the audience of 1606** would not trust them. They would be viewed as **Satanic and witch hunters would burn them to death**. Despite this, he focuses on the prophecies he likes. *Alternatively, we might* argue* that he remains a sceptic. He welcomes his good fortune, but he still knows they are untrustworthy.

Earlier, Banquo described the witches as inhuman, "**so withered and wild in their attire that look not like the inhabitants of the earth**". Shakespeare *may* do this to* create an aura of fear for his audience who would already **fear the supernatural in 1606**. Also earlier, Macbeth pleads with the weird sisters to "**stay, you imperfect speakers**". This *reveals* how he is being controlled by his ambition, as he is desperate to discover when and how he will become king. This went against **Jacobean custom, where to try to rise above your station in life was to defy God. The Great Chain of Being** meant that God chose your status for a reason. This ambition *shows* how Macbeth is stained with sin.

In conclusion, Shakespeare *portrays* Macbeth so that the audience can see his true character and ambition in this extract. In **CONTRAST**, Banquo is *portrayed* as noble, suspicious of the supernatural, and concerned at Macbeth's curiosity about the witches.

Original 561 words

22 marks

- **Thesis Statement No**
- **Explanations 12**
- **Quotes 5**
- **Named Methods 3**
- **Society/era/patriarchal/Jacobean/contemporary/ historical reference 5**
- **Shakespeare 3**
- **Exploratory Could, Might, May, Perhaps, Probably 4**
- **Conclusion Yes**
- **Paragraphs 5**
- **Words per paragraph 112**

My Comments

There it is again. The first 3 paragraphs are all about the extract. The student does this very well, and in the third paragraph they also weave in relevant context to explore Shakespeare's viewpoint.

The student deals with the later prophecies – 'the prophecies he likes' – very, very briefly. Imagine if they had dealt with a few more incidents of the supernatural in the play. This is a student who could have smashed this question.

Once again, it is an answer anchored by the extract. The 'supernatural' has meant only the witches because of this. But it could have involved:

- The dagger of the mind
- Lady Macbeth and her murdering ministers.
- Banquo's ghost!

All 3 of these could be linked to Shakespeare's ideas about divine punishment, the psychology of guilt, the desire to flatter King James, the misogynistic, patriarchal view of women.

Easy marks!

They wrote fewer than 600 words, at least 200 fewer than they could have written in the time limit.

Lazy?

Examiner Comments

- This answer is Level 5 because of the overall approach to the essay, writing about the witches in the whole play, and linking this to relevant context about how Jacobeans perceived witches.
- To improve, the student should focus more on Shakespeare's ideas, and how he presents them.

Question 1

Response 16

Macbeth is *presented* as a violent character through his thoughts, actions and the opinions of other characters.

The captain first calls Macbeth "**brave**" and "**merciless**". These *suggest* violence, *portraying* Macbeth's power as a warrior. Consequently, *we infer* his violent nature through being a soldier. His sword also "**smoked with bloody execution**". This **METAPHOR** *reveals* Macbeth's brutality as it *implies* that his sword "**smoked**" from overuse. It reeks of death. This GORY IMAGERY *emphasises* the brutality of the battle.

Macbeth further "**unseamed**" his enemy "**from the nave to th'chaps**". The verb *reveals* how this man is ripped open from his stomach to his chin. This brutality is unnecessary, so we *infer* his attraction to violence, choosing to slaughter his enemies using extreme violence. He follows this by fixing the enemy's "**head upon our battlements**". This too is extravagant violence. Macbeth uses this to incite fear, and to boast of his triumph.

Shakespeare uses Lady Macbeth to **CONTRAST** with Macbeth, *emphasising* his weakness of mind. She doesn't accept his objections to regicide, when he tells her "**We will proceed no further in this business.**" She dismisses his sense of honour and loyalty, taunting him with, "**you would be so much more the man**", and this finally convinces him. Macbeth's weakness of mind is *emphasised* by her manipulation of him. We could* argue that his previous violence was confined to battle, rather than a desire to kill.

Macbeth's thoughts are also focused on violence, as he says "**let not light see my black and deep desires**". This **CONTRAST** of light with darkness *illustrates* the sinister nature of Macbeth's "**desires**". He wants to hide these desires because they are so sinful and brutal. This *suggests* his thoughts are even more violent than his previous actions. This is *reinforced* by his statement that "**present fears are less than horrible imaginings**". This internal vision of the violence Macbeth imagines himself committing affects him physically, so that Banquo asks him if he is well. This *implies* the extremity of his violent desires.

The contemporary audience would already have been shocked by the witches, and would now be horrified that Macbeth, who was not shocked by them, has imagined "**dark desires**" which are so violent as to shock himself. The violence of then murdering king Duncan leads to a descent into deception and lies. Jacobeans believed in the Great Chain of Being as the natural order. Consequently, the murder of the king must result in chaos. Macbeth's violence therefore feels even more extreme as it destroys this natural order.

Macbeth commits a series of murders due to his ambition, killing his friend Banquo and the family of the fleeing Macduff. These murders fail to give him a sense of security, *revealing* that his violence was unnecessary. Macbeth's paranoia leads to his attempt to have Fleance killed. He reacts to his failure with "**We have scorched the snake, not killed it**", which *reveals* that he sees Fleance as a "**snake**" to be disposed of. He no longer values the lives of others. *We understand* that he seems addicted to violence and murder, as his actions become more extreme.

Macbeth's violent thoughts lead him to madness, as he tells his wife, "**Full of scorpions is my mind**!" Scorpions violently inflict pain, just as Macbeth's desires do. Consequently we *understand* the fragility of Macbeth's sanity, as his own mind *appears to* cause him pain and fear. These thoughts of violence *appear to* have overtaken his mind with darkness.

At the beginning of the play, Macbeth was an example of respected manhood, a warrior who was successful in battle. He gained respect from the king through his violence and success. This violence was used positively, so Duncan puts his "**absolute trust**" in Macbeth, which

Original 861 words

24 marks

- **Thesis Statement Yes**
- **Explanations 19**
- **Quotes 13**
- **Named Methods 3**
- **Society/era/patriarchal/Jacobean/contemporary/ historical reference etc 4**
- **Shakespeare 1**
- **Exploratory Could, Might, May, Perhaps, Probably 1**
- **Conclusion Yes**
- **Paragraphs 9**
- **Words per paragraph 96**

My Comments

What I love most about this answer is the ending. This student knows that, if they stop writing, they are throwing away marks. And slow writing will also throw away marks. This is why they have stopped mid-sentence, when they have been told to put pens down!

They understand they are being chased by a T Rex on roller skates, and the only way to slow it down is to keep dropping pearls of wisdom. Words, words, words – 861 of them.

There is a thesis statement. But it would have been so much better if it dealt with Shakespeare's reasons for presenting the character of Macbeth in these ways.

This might have got into the top band if it had been planned chronologically. Almost every paragraph here stands on its own. Only the first two after the thesis statement have to go together. You could chop the essay up, stick the paragraphs in a different order, and it would still make just as much sense.

That is not an argument, it is a list of ideas. That happens because you start with the extract.

Examiner Comments
- The answer links the effects of "smoked" to violence. By this point, the essay has reached Level 4 for AO2.
- By the end of paragraph 6 the essay has reached Level 4 for AO1 References.
- It has focused very well on ideas.
- The analysis of the imagery of light is Level 5 for AO2 and AO1.
- There is not enough about how violence is linked to Jacobean ideas about masculinity for Level 5 AO3.
- Overall, this is a thoughtful and developed essay.

Question 1

Response 17

<u>Shakespeare</u> *portrays* Macbeth as violent for several purposes. His violent actions are respected by his peers and Duncan. His ambition and guilt also cause him to become more violent in his language. However, his violence is encouraged and developed most by the powerful women of the play, Lady Macbeth and the witches.

The extract *portrays* Macbeth as a violent warrior, as he is praised as "**brave Macbeth – well he deserves that name**". This *implies* that a <u>Jacobean audience</u> valued violence, strength and valour, and saw these as signs of masculinity. <u>**Men had a duty to dominate, which differs from a modern perspective**</u>. *We can see this* dominance when Macbeth is described fighting "**with his brandished steel, which smoked with bloody execution**". This steaming sword is *portrayed* violently as smoking with the blood of his victims.

The strength of "**steel**" is a **SYMBOL** for Macbeth's strength in mastering this "**bloody**" weapon, which further *emphasises* his violence. The manner in which he killed Macdonwald where "**he unseamed him from the nave to th'chaps**" makes killing *appear* easy. This level of ruthless violence might* horrify <u>a modern audience</u> as he butchers his enemy. We would also be horrified that he is rewarded for this with the title "Thane of Cawdor". However, perhaps* <u>Shakespeare</u> was keen to *portray* Macbeth as <u>a Jacobean role model</u> of masculine strength. This will make his audience sympathetic to his downfall, because Macbeth fulfils <u>**society's expectations**</u>.

After killing Duncan, Macbeth suffers from guilt. This leads to both physical and verbal violence, *which we see* in his first reaction to Lady Macbeth's death. The souring of their relationship is *reflected* in his statement, "**she should have died hereafter**". His harsh, emotionless tone *reveals* how guilt has caused his mind to stop functioning normally. This will also lead to violence. His attitude **CONTRASTS** to the equality they shared at the beginning of the play when he called her "**my dearest partner of greatness**". But Macbeth's guilt at his own violence has ruined this.

It is also a **CONTRAST** to the way Macduff responds to the death of his wife: "**But I must also feel it as a man.**" <u>Shakespeare</u> makes Macduff focus on how he must "**feel**" in order to *reveal* his emotions and *show* how his first reaction is not to turn to violence. So we *understand* that Macbeth chose violence as a consequence of his ambition.

In addition, his violent actions towards Banquo have been encouraged by his wife, who had feared Macbeth was "**too full o' th' milk of human kindness**". This *illustrates* how she believes Macbeth needs to <u>**conform to masculine norms**</u> by becoming less kind and more violent. *We imagine* Macbeth as pure and innocent through the comparison to "**milk**", *implying* that Macbeth is not strong enough to commit violence in order to fulfil his ambition of being king. This *may* explain* why she asks the supernatural to "**unsex**" her. She can be Macbeth's cruelty, but to do this she decides to emasculate him. She therefore begins to instruct him, "**sleek o'er your rugged looks/Be bright and jovial**", which tells him to become positive rather than negative. This also introduces the **THEME** of appearance and reality.

Macbeth has a violent curiosity, *which we see* when he returns to the witches and demands to know more, saying "**But one word more**" and "**tell me more**". We become unsympathetic towards him because he feeds his violent ambition. The witches are not **typical of Jacobean women**, who would be submissive. Instead, they use Macbeth's status and violence to achieve their own form of power.

Consequently, Shakespeare doesn't just *show* that bravery and ambition combine to cause Macbeth's violence. He also *shows* that the witches, as powerful women, create his violence, so that Shakespeare can explore the **role of women in Jacobean society**.

Original 855 words

25 marks

- **Thesis Statement Yes**
- **Explanations 22**
- **Quotes 11**
- **Named Methods 4**
- **Society/era/patriarchal/Jacobean/contemporary/ historical reference etc 9**
- **Shakespeare 5**
- **Exploratory Could, Might, May, Perhaps, Probably 3**
- **Conclusion Yes**
- **Paragraphs 8**
- **Words per paragraph 107**

My Comments

Ok, this is a potential grade 9 essay.

But the student fails to write about Shakespeare's purposes or ideas in the thesis statement. It would have been such an easy fix. You can bet they knew those ideas!

The extract is dealt with quickly, in two paragraphs, so the student can write about the rest of the play. Because the extract is in the first Act, it is easy to work through the play chronologically, to write an argument.

Instead, though, the student doesn't. They link the paragraphs about Lady Macbeth and Lady Macduff well, but the rest could go in any order.

Had they dealt with Lady Macbeth's encouragement of violence in the killing of Banquo *first*, the student could then have traced this as a cause of the later rift in the marriage. This consequence of violence would then have formed part of an argument which shows violence turning against its perpetrators. This links to Shakespeare's cautionary tale, and therefore to a higher grade. This is so obvious that even the examiner is going to notice it – see their last bullet point below.

Why settle for 25 marks, when a slight change can get you 30?

Examiner Comments
- You can see how the answer begins as a good explained response for Level 3.
- But by the end it has become detailed and developed.
- The first three paragraphs deal with implicit or abstract ideas, like ambition, guilt and bravery.
- The answer becomes clearly Level 4 when the student writes about Macbeth being a victim of society's expectations.
- The comments about Macduff move into Level 5, as they are thoughtful.
- The analysis of the word 'milk' takes the answer further into Level 5.
- By the end of the answer, all the AOs are in Level 5.
- To improve, the student should think about how Shakespeare constructs the text to deliver his ideas.

Level 6

Convincing, critical analysis and exploration 26 – 30 marks Grade 9

Marks	Words	Thesis	Exp.	Quote	Methods	Context	Shake	Exp L	Conc.	Para
26	617	Y	19	10	9	8	11	1	Y	8
30	663	Y	21	10	8	5	7	3	Y	7
30	1250	Y	24	12	4	5	6	0	Y	10
30	1139	Y	27	11	7	12	14	5	Y	10
30	1206	Y	20	21	10	13	6	4	Y	10
Ave	975	Y	22	13	8	9	9	3	Y	9

Question 2

Response 18

Shakespeare portrays Lady Macbeth as ultimately consumed by her guilt, as a result of her manipulation of Macbeth. She schemed to make him commit treason and regicide.

Shakespeare's **REPETITION** of "**Out, damned spot. Out I say!**" *emphasises* the effects of the "**blood**" they have spilled. Lady Macbeth's conscience can't handle her horrifying thoughts, which *implies* she can't go back. Shakespeare *illustrates* how a person can be damaged by encouraging or committing murder. Alternatively, this "**spot**" *could* be a SYMBOL* of evil, marking her as a witch. **A Jacobean audience** would have believed witches had a similar "**damned spot**" on their bodies, *as SYMBOLS* of their demonic "**spirits**". This sinister image *suggests* Lady Macbeth is a wicked woman, an eerie character.

Moreover, Shakespeare *portrays* Lady Macbeth as tortured by their **treasonous regicide**. He uses further images of "**blood**" which even all the perfumes of Arabia will "**not sweeten this little hand**" of hers. **JUXTAPOSING** "**perfumes**", which cause delight, with "**blood**" and the "disease" of sleepwalking creates a mysterious **CONTRAST**. Shakespeare *portrays* Lady Macbeth as tortured and seriously uneasy. This *emphasises* the negativity of her transformation, which was caused by her unchecked ambition and her violence.

In this extract, Shakespeare also explores the **THEME** of deception. Lady Macbeth *appears* to need to convince herself to act: "**look not so pale**". These **MONOSYLLABLES** build up a rhythm, and the momentum is continued with "**wash your hands**". *She is trying* to rid herself of her memories of regicide. However, Shakespeare uses **DRAMATIC IRONY** with her references to "**blood**". *We know* this is not a physical presence she can wash away, but a **METAPHOR** of her psychological and spiritual struggle to overcome her conscience and knowledge that her sins are unforgivable. This **MONOSYLLABIC** phrasing *conveys* how her regrets now overwhelm her thoughts and conscience.

At the start of the play Shakespeare characterises Lady Macbeth as willing to unbalance **the natural order** in pursuit of her ambition to be queen. He *portrays* her as powerful when she commands "**unsex me here**". He *reveals* that she feels the need to adopt a male role as **men are dominant in this patriarchal society**. She wants to have the strength males have in committing murder and treason. **A Jacobean audience** would be stunned by her ability to wield the power of a man, as **women in society** were considered weak.

Shakespeare *emphasises* her power through her statement, "**when you durst do it, then you were a man**". By criticising his masculinity, Lady Macbeth persuades Macbeth to **treason and regicide**. Shakespeare *portrays* her power as negative and impossible to control, as she manipulates Macbeth.

The **SEMANTIC FIELD** of evil "**spirits**" *implies* that Lady Macbeth is a **follower of Satan**. She has been possessed by the devil. This causes nature to reject her, so that she is denied the natural power of sleep.

Shakespeare *emphasises* the **CYCLICAL** character of her journey, with the phrase "**golden round**". She loses all her power and becomes consumed by guilt. Shakespeare warns against **regicide** by *exploring* the consequences of her ambition, guilt and pursuit of power.

Original 617 words

26 marks

- Thesis Statement Yes
- Explanations 19
- Quotes 10
- Named Methods 9
- Society/era/patriarchal/Jacobean/contemporary/ historical reference etc 8
- Shakespeare 11

- **Exploratory Could, Might, May, Perhaps, Probably 1**
- **Conclusion Yes**
- **Paragraphs 8**
- **Words per paragraph 77**

My Comments

Look, my version of this essay is 510 words long. The student's was pretty short, at 617 words. There is a huge level of skill here to earn 26 marks in such few words.

But, before we get to that, look at the thesis statement. It has 3 parts, but none of them deals with Shakespeare's purpose. That's always the easiest way to get higher grades.

The language analysis of 'Out, damned spot' is linked to more than one interpretation. Context is used to back up interpretations. This is a blueprint for how to get Level 6 for AO2 language analysis, and for AO3 context.

It upsets me that this student can score so highly when they aren't really having to write a proper essay. But I will live. Because they are able to write about the extract in so much detail, their AO2 and AO3 marks go through the roof.

If you are a knowledgeable and clever student who doesn't love English, or who doesn't want to learn to write a logical and convincing argument, this approach definitely works.

I've argued against it up to now because we can see how often it goes wrong, and limits your mark.

To be clear, it also limits this student's mark, but they are still scoring 26/30. That's the very start of grade 9! So, who cares, right?

It is also worth remembering the T Rex lumbering behind you – if this student had simply trained their writing speed, and reached 900-1000 words, they would easily have scored 30/30.

So, if you are knowledgeable and clever, starting with the extract can work. If you are knowledgeable, but not one of the cleverest people in your class, it is much easier to get grade 9 by writing an essay chronologically, with 8 paragraphs.

Examiner Comments

- The opening paragraphs shows the student has a very good understanding of the task.
- The essay starts straight in with an analysis of the symbolism of the word "spot" for very high AO2 marks.
- The analysis of monosyllabic sentences clearly links methods to Shakespeare's ideas.

- The essay mainly analyses language from the extract, which can still lead to Level 6 for AO2.
- There are enough references to the rest of the text to be developed and thoughtful.
- The thesis statement at the beginning was very helpful. The ending could have revisited that and evaluated some more of those initial ideas.

Question 1

Response 19

In this extract <u>Shakespeare</u> focuses on Macbeth's violence. This *emphasises* his bravery, which is lauded by others. It also introduces the **THEME** of masculinity, equating it to violence. Macbeth's final downfall is also **FORESHADOWED** in this extract.

<u>Shakespeare</u> *portrays* Macbeth's violence as gruesome, as "**he unseamed him from the nave to th'chaps**". He *appears* to rip Macdonwald apart. Perhaps* this *emphasises* the excessive violence Macbeth uses, in excess of that needed to kill his enemy. This **FORESHADOWS** how excessively violent he becomes later. *We see this* clearly when Macbeth then "**fixed his head upon our battlements**", because Macbeth's head is also displayed this way at the end. This **CYCLICAL ENDING** *implies* that violence must lead to a destructive cycle, and how Macbeth's own violence led to his downfall.

However, at the beginning, <u>Shakespeare</u> *presents* Macbeth's violence as both brave and noble. The Sergeant describes the battle in **EPIC** terms, so that he claims "**brave Macbeth – well he deserves that name.**" This helps *us understand* the relationship between violence and brave masculinity. So Lady Macbeth associates masculinity with violence and supernatural spirits to "**unsex me**". Next, she manipulates Macbeth to murder Duncan by insulting his masculinity as insufficiently violent. Linking violence to <u>regicide</u> could* *imply* that <u>Shakespeare</u> views masculinity as toxic.

"**Brave Macbeth**" also *reveals* that Macbeth feels most at home in battle, because he can express his violence without having to justify the morality of his brutality. This is repeated in Act V when he fights Macduff, still brave even though he knows he will be killed. He becomes once more the noble warrior we met in Act I. The *significance* of "**brave Macbeth**" would intrigue the <u>Jacobean audience</u>, as <u>Shakespeare</u> has **FIRST INTRODUCED US** to the witches who have already told us that Macbeth is their target. The audience *wonder how* the brave and noble Macbeth can be corrupted by their evil.

This extract also introduces the **MOTIF** of blood, as Macbeth's sword "**smoked with bloody execution**". This *portrays* Macbeth's violence as skilful, noble and necessary, wielded for a just cause. This **MOTIF** soon comes to *represent* Macbeth's guilt. He sees it as *SYMBOLIC* of his own crimes when he observes "**I am in blood stepped so far**".

In the extract, his violence is *portrayed* as an art form, as "**their art**". In contrast, the **SIMILE** "**as two spent swimmers that do cling together**" *implies* that this art of violence will lead to his <u>tragedy</u>. <u>Shakespeare</u> also uses **PERSONIFICATION** to link violence and <u>fate</u>, with "**Disdaining Fortune**". This is **IRONIC**, as it *implies* Macbeth can overcome his <u>fate</u>. Yet his violent acts are going to lead directly to his tragic <u>fate</u>.

To conclude, this extract *portrays* Macbeth as inherently violent, but *shows* how his violence is used in a noble cause rather than for personal ambition. This also *portrays* masculinity as inherently violent. We must also remember the **context of the Gunpower Plot**. Shakespeare's play *could* be a CAUTIONARY TALE* warning that violence will turn on the violent, leading to the fate of their own destruction.

Original 663 words

30 marks

- **Thesis Statement Yes**
- **Explanations 21**
- **Quotes 10**
- **Named Methods 8**
- **Society/era/patriarchal/Jacobean/contemporary/ historical reference etc 5**
- **Shakespeare 7**
- **Exploratory Could, Might, May, Perhaps, Probably 3**
- **Conclusion Yes**
- **Paragraphs 7**
- **Words per paragraph 95**

My Comments
Hurrah, a thesis statement in at least 3 parts which mentions Shakespeare's purpose, to explore masculinity.

The next paragraph deals with both the beginning and the ending of the play. Although this deviates from a chronological structure to your essay, it has the massive advantage of showing the examiner you are dealing with the whole play.

It also lets them know that you are constructing an argument which is going to explain the ending. The ending should always help you write about Shakespeare's purpose. Here it is the idea that violence will turn upon the violent, Macbeth's violent acts becoming bloody instruction which then turns upon him.

To be clear, writing about the ending always gets you better grades, because it always forces you to write about Shakespeare's point of view. You can, of course, do this even more easily by working through the play chronologically.

This student doesn't bother with that. Why?

They are very knowledgeable and they're clever. They know they can find so much to say about the extract. That said, it is still incredibly short. You will be much more certain of your grade if you write more.

Now, go back and look at the methods. **Cyclical, foreshadows, first introduced, motif** are all methods related to the structure of the play. Because comments about structure start at Level 5, these are really valuable methods to include.

The student also uses the same trick of comparing the beginning to the end. So they examine the change in the motif of blood, and the change from fortune to fate.

This is a clever approach, which takes practice, and relies on the ability to think very logically under exam conditions.

That's my point. Most of us can't do that. But all of us can follow our character or theme chronologically. This will always compare the beginning to the end. So we will always be in with a chance of getting grade 9.

Examiner Comments

- This essay is well structured.
- It explores ideas all the time, through several parts of the play.
- It develops a very effective argument by using lots of references.
- It links the structure of the play to ideas well for Level 5.
- By the time the student writes about 'toxic masculinity' and Macbeth's role as a soldier, the ideas are firmly Level 6.

Question 1

Response 20

Shakespeare *portrays* Macbeth's violence in this extract and the play as a whole, offering us **HYPERBOLIC** and graphic description. When faced with a problem, Macbeth's first thoughts always appear to be violent.

The captain in this extract *portrays* Macbeth wielding a sword which appears to be designed for murder, "**with his brandished steel, which smoked with bloody execution.**" The speed of his fighting is *conveyed* with "**smoked**", and the "**execution**" is so sudden that we can imagine smoke literally rising from his sword. *Our first impression* of Macbeth is that he kills enthusiastically. Its "**brandished steel**" *portrays* how well suited Macbeth is to battle, which *suggests* he has always been predisposed to violence. *We understand* that Macbeth's violence is admirable and a sign of his bravery. The effect of Macbeth's violence is to exhaust his enemies, so that they were "**as two spent swimmers that do cling together**". The verb "**cling**" *implies* their desperation.

We understand what a powerful warrior Macbeth must be, and that he uses his violent skill loyally to fight for Scotland. The captain calls him "**brave Macbeth**" to *emphasise* how his violence makes him a superior warrior. This loyalty is honourable. Shakespeare glorifies Macbeth at the **BEGINNING** of the play to prepare for the shocking **CONTRAST** of his downfall. Macbeth has a dramatic effect on others, as we see when he exhausts the army, like "**two spent swimmers**".

Initially, therefore, Macbeth's violence is a sign of his skill and loyalty to King Duncan and his desire to protect his country. The description that he "**unseamed him from the nave to th' chaps**" is graphically violent, but Macbeth's enthusiasm is *portrayed* as loyalty to Duncan. He basically rips people apart to be sure they are totally dead. He wants to be certain he has performed his role properly.

The Elizabethan belief in **the Divine Right of Kings** means that, when Macbeth is loyal to King Duncan, the audience *understand* that he is also loyal to God, who has chosen Duncan to be king. This further *portrays* Macbeth's violence as a sign of his noble loyalty, and makes him admirable. However, in the rest of the play, Macbeth's desire to murder is caused by his own ambition. Despite his noble character in Act 1, the witches' prophecies will tempt Macbeth towards evil. Initially, he tries to resist his ambition. He lists reasons why he shouldn't kill Duncan. He tries to distance himself from murder by calling it "**assassination**". This *suggests* his morality won't allow him to act without honour.

Macbeth understands his desires are evil, yet the witches are still able to persuade him to murder. Therefore, when Macbeth evaluates his morality, *we understand* that he is not attracted to violence. Shakespeare *reveals* that Macbeth knows he is hungry for power but dislikes his own desires. *We realise* that he will lose his morality.

Once Macbeth commits regicide, he turns to violence even more quickly. He regularly uses violent and murderous language. *We can see* how his thoughts become immediately violent once he has killed Duncan, when he says "**methought I heard a voice cry Macbeth doth murder sleep**," so he even imagines killing sleep. This is extremely bad, and would have shocked Shakespeare's audience. Elizabethans viewed sleep as a reward which God gave to those who were without sin and had laboured hard during the day. So Macbeth's murder of sleep *portrays* him as sinful. God is displeased because God appointed king Duncan and now Macbeth has murdered him, so he will never sleep again. Ironically this even affects Lady Macbeth. Her involvement in Duncan's murder leads to her sleep-walking. Shakespeare *presents this* as a shocking **VOLTA** in Macbeth's character.

Macbeth now lies to his close friend Banquo, and then to his wife about murdering Banquo. He has become worse. He worries about the witches' predictions and becomes increasingly paranoid. The witches tell him Banquo will get **"kings hereafter"** and they call Banquo **"lesser than Macbeth but much greater"** which *suggests* that his children will become kings. Macbeth is totally convinced by these prophecies and intends to murder Banquo. Whereas Banquo is not taken in by the prophecies as he thinks they are **"instrument of darkness"**. Macbeth is so motivated by violence that he keeps his plans secret from Lady Macbeth, isolating her: **"Be innocent of the knowledge, dearest chuck"**. So his violence and paranoia lead him on a self-destructive path. Shakespeare *shows* this violent paranoia increases after Macbeth murders Duncan.

Alternatively, *some view* Lady Macbeth as the main cause of Macbeth's violence. Her masculine cruelty and harshness remove Macbeth's doubts and uncertainties. She manipulates him by ridiculing his doubts as cowardice, even after Macbeth has tried to retain control, instructing **"We will proceed no further in this business"**. However, although "will" is an **IMPERATIVE**, it does not command Lady Macbeth, who instead sees herself as his equal. Her manipulation causes him to become paranoid and violent, which leads to his death. Her invocation of spirits to **"fill me … with direst cruelty"** *portrays* her as more evil than Macbeth, and she uses this influence to goad him to commit regicide. She is the most powerful influence on his violence.

In conclusion, Shakespeare presents Macbeth as initially moral and honourable, so only partly attracted to violence, but he loses himself as power goes to his head.

Original 1250 words

30 marks

- **Thesis Statement Yes**

- Explanations 24
- Named Methods 4
- Quotes 12
- Society/era/patriarchal/Jacobean/contemporary/ historical reference etc 5
- Exploratory Could, Might, May, Perhaps, Probably 0
- Conclusion Yes
- Shakespeare 6
- Paragraphs 10
- Words per paragraph 125

My Comments

This student is *not* one of the cleverest students in their class. They don't know that Macbeth is also one of the "two spent swimmers". They don't know that in 1605 England is Jacobean, and that this is no longer a Tudor monarchy. They slip in some very sloppy vocabulary – 'this is extremely bad'. My version is 887 words compared to their original 1250 words, which means that it was 29% waffle!

So, how did they get such high marks?

They wrote a huge number of words, with a tonne of explanations. Points make prizes.

Once they finished with the extract, they just wrote about as many quotes as they could think about. They realised that this did not always stick to the question, so they added to their analysis with the equivalent of 'and this links to violence because'.

The analysis is grade 9 because the student keeps looking at the changes in Macbeth. They link these to abstract ideas like morality, sin, bravery. They use context as much as possible to back up their interpretations.

This is my favourite answer so far because it teaches three principles I teach all my students:

1. Getting top grades is just knowing stuff (which is just effort)

2. Write like you are being chased by T Rex hungry for words (which is just effort)

3. 50% of students could get grades 7+ if they did this.

Examiner Comments

- The essay jumps straight in to some language analysis of 'smoked with bloody execution' and this is a Level 5 example.
- By the end of the fourth paragraph, the answer has explored lots of ideas in a thoughtful and detailed way, for Level 5.

- The paragraph dealing with loyalty and violence has lifted the whole answer into Level 5.
- The essay is exploratory also when it deals with the rest of the play. Writing about Jacobean perspectives of violence means that it is Level 6 for AO3, even though the student thinks it is Elizabethan.
- By the end, every AO is Level 6, and the effects of language have been explored for AO2.

Question 4

Response 21

Shakespeare *portrays* the supernatural as an attack on morality. The witches **subvert morality**, play on Macbeth's weaknesses and manipulate him. They are the **CATALYST** for his downfall.

In the extract Shakespeare *emphasises* Banquo's concerns about the witches. He observes "**tis strange**" after he has met them. Next, he views them as objects, as "**instruments**". Perhaps* this **FORESHADOWS** how they will use the play's protagonists as instruments, or puppets, later in the play. This is *amplified* when the witches are related to "**darkness**", which *indicates* their evil nature. Shakespeare may* be *indicating* that their evil is not all powerful, that the supernatural can be resisted, and that Macbeth chooses to follow an evil path of his own free will.

In this extract *we can see* that the supernatural are a **CATALYST**. Their prophesies generate both Macbeth's eagerness and his guilt. Shakespeare *illustrates* this by dramatising Macbeth's indecision in the extract, where he can't explore the consequences of their prophecies which "**cannot be ill, cannot be good**". This language echoes the **PARADOX** of "**fair is foul and foul is fair**" at the start of the play. This *reveals* how the witches subvert **moral viewpoints.** It also *develops* the major **THEME** of appearance and reality, caused by the supernatural.

Through Macbeth's actions, Shakespeare warns that those who are tempted by the supernatural will be consumed and destroyed by them. The supernatural incubate in Macbeth both his extreme ambition, and then his guilt, both of which lead to his **tragic downfall**. Shakespeare *emphasises* this though Banquo who rejects acting on the witches' prophesies, explaining that they will have "**deepest consequences**". This *conveys* how people can freely choose to reject the temptation of the supernatural.

Macbeth describes his temptation as "**against the use of nature**". This **FORESHADOWS** how he will destroy the **natural order, committing a crime against God and the Divine Right of Kings** by committing **regicide**. Shakespeare uses this **FORESHADOWING** to *portray* Macbeth as naïve to the power and manipulation of the witches, and naïve to how easily he is tempted.

Throughout the play, Shakespeare uses the supernatural, and Macbeth and Banquo's reactions to it, to hook his audience. This is why **THE PLAY BEGINS** with the witches, and why they begin with a question, "**When shall we three meet again?**" The **Jacobean fascination with witchcraft and superstition** is instantly engaged. Shakespeare *shows* that **society** is acted on by supernatural powers, and that these lead to a person's downfall.

Perhaps* Shakespeare warns his audience to resist their own curiosity about the supernatural. His play *illustrates* how we are free to **resist the temptations of evil, through Christian faith**.

Shakespeare chose to perform the witches with actors who were older men. He *tells us this* through Banquo's description of their appearance, "**You are women, yet your beards forbid me to interpret you so**". This could* *highlight* the problems of a **patriarchal society**. Shakespeare may* be criticising how **only men in Jacobean society can achieve power, while women are victims of inequality and a lack of education**. This *explains* why these witches have turned to the supernatural in order to achieve power over others.

An alternative interpretation is that Shakespeare supports the **misogyny of the time**. The witches describe themselves as "**the weird sisters, hand in hand**", which *reveals* how women rely on each other, and have chosen to become evil. *We can also see* that Macbeth is entirely controlled by their powers. His consuming ambition *means* that he trusts in them completely. He refuses to see their part in exploiting his ambition. Therefore, as he becomes more tyrannical and paranoid, he still turns to them and their apparitions. Shakespeare explores the **THEME** of appearance and reality again.

Macbeth is made to feel falsely secure when they tell him "**none of woman born shall harm Macbeth**". They *appear to claim* he cannot be defeated. Macbeth trusts this completely. He threatens them with an "**eternal curse**" if they don't tell him what they know. This also *suggests* that Macbeth believes he has inherited the witches' ability to summon evil, by being able to summon a curse. This is similar to Lady Macbeth who instructed the "**spirits that tend on mortal thoughts**", and commanded night to "**come**" and create "**the blanket of the dark**".

In conclusion, both the protagonists are deceived by the supernatural into accepting the appearance of security. However, they are blind to the reality of their own weaknesses Macbeth is consumed by ambition and his mistaken belief that he is invincible. Lady Macbeth is initially blind to her feelings of guilt. This blindness leads to their downfalls. Shakespeare *shows* how the supernatural can manipulate our weaknesses. Macbeth is captivated while Banquo remains doubtful. This *demonstrates* that **we are all free to resist the temptation of the supernatural.**

Original 1139 words

30 marks

- **Thesis Statement Yes**
- **Explanations 27**
- **Quotes 11**
- **Named Methods 7**

- Society/era/patriarchal/Jacobean/contemporary/ historical reference 12
- Shakespeare 14
- Exploratory Could, Might, May, Perhaps, Probably 5
- Conclusion Yes
- Paragraphs 10
- Words per paragraph 114

My Comments

This is the first *essay* in the guide. It isn't just an answer. This is what writing an essay looks like. Before 2015, all literature students were taught to write actual essays.

In 2012, English Literature was the number 1 choice for students taking A level. This was a reason why. Writing an essay is rewarding in itself – it's not just for the exam. Writing a coherent, logical argument, is a transferrable life skill.

But, by 2022, English was only the 12th most popular choice. Students now take up sociology and psychology instead. And this is one reason why – we teach students really shoddy ways to write, so they don't see the value in the subject.

As teachers, we are robbing students of this vital life skill. After all, if you can't sequence your ideas to write a logical argument, who is going to bother listening to them?

If you learn to write an essay, it is going to be impossible to get less than a grade 7!

1. It starts with a 4 part thesis statement.

2. It deals with the play chronologically. (It's helped by the extract coming very early in the play).

3. It treats the supernatural as just the witches, but follows them chronologically.

4. The conclusion links to the ending of the play, and the characters.

You'll notice the usual skills of top grade essays –

- Analyse as many quotes as you can.
- Write as many explanations as you can.
- Concentrate on how characters change.
- Use lots of context to back up your interpretation.
- Have alternative interpretations.
- Always link interpretations to the author's purpose.

How many of these can you already do?

Examiner Comments

- This is conceptualised from the start because it begins with a thesis.
- The rest of the essay then goes on to explore the ideas in the thesis.
- The student chooses really good references and quotes to fit their argument.
- Context is always used like a quote, as evidence to back up an interpretation.
- This essay is better than full marks.
- Hardly any 16 year old will write like this. *The examiner actually pointed that out.*

(But that doesn't mean you couldn't – it just means that teachers aren't teaching their students to write this well, because they aren't taught to write an actual essay. I hope you now can)

Question 3

Response 22

In Shakespeare's Macbeth, the relationship between the tragic hero and his "**fiend-like queen**" is *portrayed* as ambiguous. **The conventional perspective** is that Lady Macbeth emasculates her husband, provoking him through jibes and cruelty, domineering him so that he will commit the inconceivable crime of **regicide**. This is an attack on **nature and God**. *This interpretation* looks at Lady Macbeths flawed character which unbalances power in their relationship. However, *an alternative interpretation suggests* that they are united by love, and so their marriage defies **Jacobean social norms**. This would *mean* that the imbalance of power in their relationship is simply a moment in the natural rhythm of loving marriages.

Shakespeare uses the **Biblical SYMBOLISM of Original Sin** to link Macbeth and Lady Macbeth to **Adam and Eve**, through the instruction "**look like the innocent flower but be the serpent under it**". Just like **Adam and Eve in Genesis**, Macbeth and Lady Macbeth support each other in their sin against God. They "**cling**" to each other like the "**two spent swimmers**" in the battle described by the Captain in Act 1.

Their relationship deteriorates as Macbeth becomes more addicted to violence. Instead of seeking advice from Lady Macbeth, he turns instead to the "**weird sisters**", even though he knows their predictions make them "**imperfect speakers**". This *suggests* his severance of intimacy and influence leads to her madness in Act 5.

Although guilt drives her to madness, her suicide is because she has been spurned. Where once he called her "**dearest chuck**", he has now stopped depending on her. Shakespeare uses an intertextual **MOTIF** *to show* how she has depended on Macbeth. In Act 2, Macbeth exclaimed that "**all great Neptune's oceans**" could not clean Duncan's blood from his hands. Lady Macbeth echoes this **MOTIF** when she imagines a "**spot**" of blood which not even "**perfumes**" from Arabia can disguise.

One interpretation is that her suicidal feelings are caused, not be her own guilt, but by taking on Macbeth's guilt. She may* do this out of love for him. This *is further hinted* at when she does not simply stop at Duncan. His blood was literally on her hands after she replaced the daggers. But she also references Banquo and the innocent "**wife**" of "**The Thane of Fife**". She takes on Macbeth's guilt for these murders also.

The **SEMANTIC FIELDS** also *reveal* a misogynistic split in the marriage. Shakespeare references **classical literature** through the **Roman God Neptune**, while lady Macbeth references nothing more serious than "**perfumes**". This **CONTRAST** *emphasises* the **Jacobean dismissal of women** as shallow, in **CONTRAST** to men who wrestle with timeless knowledge and action. Shakespeare also uses this **JUXTAPOSITION** to show that Macbeth is superior in other ways. Lady Macbeth only cares for the "**crown**", the here and now, whereas Macbeth is concerned with his legacy, the sweep of history, and fathering heirs.

Another way of analysing these differences is *to see them* as proof of a deep connection between Lady Macbeth and Macbeth. Consequently, in the extract, Lady Macbeth expresses almost a parent's love for her husband. Her reprimand "**tis the eye of childhood / That fears a painted devil**" doesn't just dismiss and insult him as a silly child, it also *suggests* she loves him as a child. Although she knows he has earned martial glory in battle, she also <u>understands</u> that, like a child, he is "**infirm of purpose**". So, like a mother, she takes control here, and takes the daggers to "**gild the faces**" of the grooms, to correct Macbeth's childish mistake. Lady Macbeth's pride in her husband for killing Duncan, and in her own execution of her plan, is *revealed* in the verb "**gild**". She associates "**blood**" with the securing of a gilded future as queen. <u>Shakespeare</u> therefore *portrays* her as a flawed maternal character who will become the "**fiend-like queen**".

Many critics view her as the antithesis of motherhood. So she replaces her mother's "**milk**" and Macbeths "**milk of human kindness**" with poisonous "**gall**" in her famous **SOLILOQUY**. She rejects the <u>convention of a mother nurturing her family</u>, and instead decides to poison her husband with her "**spirits**". Perhaps* Macbeth's "**black and deep desires**" are not just to assassinate Duncan, but to see his wife as a motherly figure, so that <u>like Hamlet</u>, his <u>desires are Oedipal</u>.

We can even go so far as to *suggest* that Lady Macbeth's "**keen knife**" and "**the wound it makes**" is a subtle **ALLUSION** to <u>Caesarean section, which would have killed the mother</u>, just as she kills her own feminine motherly role. Even "**the blanket of the dark**" might* **SYMBOLISE** the dark protection of the womb. Later Scotland is described as "**entombed**" in "**darkness**", and <u>Shakespeare</u> may* be using *this SYMBOL to suggest* that Scotland has been trapped **METAPHORICALLY** in Lady Macbeth's poisoned womb, nurtured only with "**direst cruelty**". Shockingly, instead of birthing life, she creates only death.

We can argue that, having lost her own child, she instead treats her husband as a child, and gives birth to <u>regicide</u>. She wants both her husband and Scotland to share an <u>Oedipal desire</u> for her. <u>Shakespeare</u> gives Macbeth a direct **REFERENCE** to <u>Oedipus Rex</u> when he wants to "**pluck out mine eyes**", *suggesting* that he also sees himself as an <u>Oedipal</u> figure in his love of his wife. This might* contribute to Lady Macbeth's strong feelings of love for him, even after he has ceased intimacies with her. Although this relationship is unbalanced and perverse, it is complex, loving and ambitious.

Original 1206 words

30 marks

- **Thesis Statement Yes**

- **Explanations 20**
- **Quotes 21**
- **Named Methods 10**
- **Society/era/patriarchal/Jacobean/contemporary/ historical reference 13**
- **Shakespeare 6**
- **Exploratory Could, Might, May, Perhaps, Probably 4**
- **Conclusion Yes**
- **Paragraphs 10**
- **Words per paragraph 120**

Examiner Comments

This is beyond GCSE standard.

My Comments

What the examiner means here is that this is better than you need to be to get 30/30.

There is a level of knowledge most schools don't teach – Oedipus Rex for example, and Freud's Oedipus complex – but that comes only at the end of the essay. If we took that knowledge out, it would still score 30/30, and still be beyond GCSE standard.

The explanation of motherhood is the best I have ever read. I would bet a lot of money that this was written by an adult, possibly a teacher, trying to find out how to help their students do better under exam conditions.

Why is it beyond GCSE standard?

- Because it is written as an essay.
- IT DOES NOT START WITH THE EXTRACT!
- It is an argument about whether the marriage shows a deteriorating relationship, or whether the Macbeth's always love each other.

You could do that, couldn't you?

You don't have to do that as well as this student, because you don't need more than 30/30.

Other Questions

How does Shakespeare present Macbeth's fears?

Response 23

We know from the moment that Macbeth receives the Weird Sisters' prophecies that he is captivated by the idea of becoming king. Lady Macbeth observes that he is just missing "**the illness that should attend**" his desires, to turn them into actions which will make him king. This **METAPHOR** is delivered in a **SOLILOQUY** once she learns of the witches' prophecies. She *highlights* Macbeth's "**ambition**", but regrets his lack of typical male qualities which would give him the necessary courage to commit regicide.

Perhaps* this *suggests* that Macbeth is initially held back by his fears. This is also *emphasised* by his reaction once he has assassinated the king. Next his fear returns, this time of Banquo and his heirs, because the witches promised them kingship. Macbeth now claims "**There is none but he/ Whose being I do fear**". This naming of his fear *suggests* that he feels insecure. His solution is to use his free will to challenge the prophecy. Shakespeare's Jacobean audience would be horrified that Macbeth has been tempted by the supernatural into pursuing his own desires by attacking **the Divine Right of Kings.**

King James' book made clear that witches were evil. So when Macbeth is so determined to follow the prophecies of these "**imperfect speakers**", the Jacobeans would be alarmed. They would expect Macbeth to share their fear of the witches, and for him to be alarmed at the consequences of acting on their words.

Macbeth complains that assassinating Duncan has "**Put rancours in the vessel of my peace**". This *implies* that Macbeth has begun to realise that he has destroyed his own peace of mind, and he fears this is the consequence the murder. A possible* interpretation is that this also *reveals* Macbeth's sense of guilt. "**Vessel**" here could remind us of blood, and blood symbolises guilt in the rest of the play. Shakespeare's audience would expect Macbeth to fear the "**deep damnation**" of killing Duncan, and therefore expect him to feel guilt.

Macbeth's fears of losing the throne keep growing, until he kills the innocent Lady Macduff and all her children. Macbeth's fear and ambition combine to make him an evil tyrant, and so he has the "**wife and babes savagely slaughtered**". The brutality of this killing is *emphasised* through the **SIBILANCE**. Macbeth's fear has also made him merciless, as *revealed* by the adverb "**savagely**". To the Jacobean audience, this would be a direct consequence of Macbeth's dealings with the supernatural.

Moreover, their horror at Macbeth's **regicide** would be increased by his decision to slaughter an innocent family who posed no threat to him. His reckless savagery *implies* that his fear has caused him to lose control. Perhaps* Macbeth has become consumed by his desire for the status of kingship. He so fears a life without this power that he will do anything to preserve his ambition.

In conclusion, Shakespeare has taken the two qualities of fear and ambition which can be positive traits, and dramatised their negativity through the character of Macbeth. Macbeth's **tragedy** is that a fear of the supernatural would have saved him. However, his fear of not being crowned, and then of losing his kingship was greater than this, causing him to become a merciless killer.

23 marks

Original 668 words

- Thesis Statement No
- Explanations 9
- Quotes 8
- Named Methods 2
- Society/era/patriarchal/Jacobean/contemporary/ historical reference etc 8
- Shakespeare 2
- Exploratory Could, Might, May, Perhaps, Probably 3
- Conclusion Yes
- Paragraphs 7

My Comments

How would this answer be turned into a grade 9? You should be able to predict what I am going to say.

- Write a thesis statement to explain Shakespeare's 3 big ideas.
- Write another 400 words.
- Find another 5 -7 quotations to write about.
- Write another 10 explanations about them, linking them to Shakespeare's ideas.

This essay shows brilliant revision. The student has pretty much prepared an essay on ambition in advance.

Then they've just seen how often they can change the word 'ambition', and replace it with the word 'fear'.

Examiner Comment
- The answer deals with fear from the very first line, so it will be a precise focus of the essay.
- They choose appropriate references from the whole play and from the extract.
- The answer deals very well with Shakespeare's ideas. The best example is how fear is linked to ambition.
- The references from the text support the student's interpretations very effectively.
- This is confident and thorough.
- To get to the top of Level 5, the answer could explore more of the methods Shakespeare used to present Macbeth's fears.

What Next?
If you aren't using this guide to write your own answers, are you making the most of it?
Why not take this essay, and rewrite to get grade 9?

How does Shakespeare present the theme of ambition in the play?

Response 24

Shakespeare *reveals* ambition as the dominant theme in the play, because it is Macbeth's overpowering ambition which leads to his immoral murder of King Duncan. Lady Macbeth and the witches can only influence Macbeth in this because his ambition is already so great.

In this extract, Shakespeare *explores* how ambition influences even the most honourable. This is why he gives Lady Macbeth the perspective that Macbeth's character is "**too full o'th' milk of human kindness**", which is her real perception because Shakespeare *reveals* it in **SOLILOQUY**. We associate "**milk**" with innocence and purity, which *implies* that Macbeth is too noble to act on his ambition. Yet, once he has reigned as king, he is viewed as a "**butcher**", because he has become both cruel and indiscriminate in his killing.

This change from excessive kindness to tyranny is a surprising journey, which warns the audience of the danger of ambition. Moreover, Shakespeare *portrays* ambition as a force which will overcome morality and reason. He gives Lady Macbeth the view that Macbeth is "**not without ambition, but without the illness should attend it**". The **COMPARISON** of ambition to "**illness**" *implies* that it is destructive, and also that this destruction can turn on the ambitious person themselves, attacking their sense of morality and ability to be kind.

Macbeth lists every reason not to murder Duncan, before focusing on his "**vaulting ambition**". This **METAPHOR** *implies* that his ambition is more powerful than his conscience, so he will overcome his moral objections.

Banquo is also **CONTRASTED** to Macbeth. They both hear the witches' prophecies. Macbeth believes all their prophecies must be true as soon as the first one is proved true when he becomes a new Thane. This belief leads to acting on his ambition to be king. However, Banquo also believes in the witches' prophecies but refuses to act on his ambitions, even once Macbeth has become king. He reacts to this critically, fearing Macbeth "**play'dst most foully for't**". This deliberately **CONTRASTS** their reactions to their ambition.

The **BINARY STRUCTURE** of the play also *illustrates* the destructive effect of ambition, focusing first on Macbeth's rise and secondly on his downfall. The lesson for <u>the audience</u> is that Macbeth's <u>tragedy</u> would have been prevented if he had learned to control his ambition, and therefore they too should learn this control.

In conclusion, Shakespeare *portrays* ambition as a destructive force which will overpower morality and reason, and lead to inevitable downfall. This is a cautionary <u>**warning to any in the audience contemplating regicide of King James**</u>.

25 marks

Original 503 words

My version is only 420 words long!

- **Thesis Statement Yes**
- **Explanations 9**
- **Quotes 5**
- **Named Methods 5**
- **Society/era/patriarchal/Jacobean/contemporary/ historical reference etc 3**
- **Shakespeare 4**
- **Exploratory Could, Might, May, Perhaps, Probably 0**
- **Conclusion Yes**
- **Paragraphs 7**

My Comments

Well, well, well. I was not expecting that mark. It doesn't have anywhere near the number of references or quotations I was expecting for AO1.

- It introduces the idea that ambition will affect 'reason', but never actually proves it – there are many easy examples and quotes revealing the mental state of Macbeth – is this a dagger, murdered sleep, never shake they gory locks, my mind is full of scorpions etc - and Lady Macbeth sleepwalking.
- The original essay included mistakes in identifying adverbs and nouns, which I've got rid of, because even naming them correctly adds no marks.
- There is very little context used to back up interpretations.

So, what has impressed the examiner?

- There are both a thesis statement and a conclusion, so it becomes a well-constructed argument.
- The student has quoted from the end of the play right at the beginning, to show that they are dealing with the whole text.
- **Although they don't give many examples from the rest of the play, they do move through it chronologically, so it is a well-constructed argument. I told you this works!**
- This, and very specific language to describe it, helps the student look at Macbeth's character arc, his 'journey', showing how Macbeth changes.
- The answer looks at the structure of the play in two ways. First by viewing Macbeth's life in two parts – a rise and fall. Secondly, by exploring Banquo as the antithesis to

Macbeth in his ambition. These two ideas mark the answer out as thoughtful and different from most students' essays.

It may be significant that this comes from 2017, which was the fist year of this GCSE. The other examples in this guide suggest that the examiners now expect more, especially for AO1.

But, English is subjective, and it is possible that this answer would still score 25 today.

Examiner Comments

- The answer focuses on ambition right from the start and with every point.
- The thesis statement and next paragraph make it clear that the student is dealing with the whole text.
- The essay is thoughtful and developed.
- The student embeds quotations and references to illustrate their ideas.
- The student's comments about Shakespeare's intentions throughout the essay show that they realise his choices are deliberate.
- In order to get into level 6 the student should explore more of Shakespeare's ideas.

Next Steps
- Write down the other ideas you could put into this essay.
- Find references or quotes to back these up.
- Write another 350 words to add in to get 30/30.

Anonymous Student Essay in My Substack Newsletter

How Does Shakespeare Present the Supernatural in Macbeth?

Response 25

Whilst the supernatural can be deemed as largely influential in Macbeth's downfall, the "**weird sisters'**" AMBIGUITY throughout the play, as well as their struggle for power in a <u>patriarchal society</u>, suggest <u>Shakespeare</u> may* not have included the supernatural in his play <u>**just to appease King James I, who was his patron**</u>. <u>Shakespeare</u> was more interested in the psychology of the characters: the supernatural witches were simply a SYMBOL of temptation that Macbeth was consumed by.

<u>Shakespeare</u> introduces the witches in the very first scene of the play which gives them large STRUCURAL significance. They chant **"Fair is foul and foul is fair"**. This PARADOXICAL CHIASMUS is a logical inconsistency that *introduces* the play's strong underlying theme of corruption and the supernatural. The witches speak in TROCHAIC TETRAMETER which distinguishes them from the other characters who typically speak in IAMBIC PENTAMETER. This would unsettle a <u>Jacobean audience</u> who were largely scared of the supernatural. <u>**King James was especially interested in it - shown by his book Daemonologie and the witch hunts he organised**</u>. The weird sisters continue to use equivocation, declaring **"when the battle's lost and won"**, unsettling the audience with its AMBIGUITY by flipping the conventional order of **"won"** first. This *alludes* to the idea of Macbeth's downfall coming first.

However, <u>Shakespeare</u> could* be diminishing the influence of the witches in the events of the play as they speak in an almost childlike manner due to their SHORT SENTENCES, SIMPLE RHYMES and CHORAL SPEECH, as if* they were children playing a game. This undermines their credibility as it *shows* the audience their game does not have any real power; they only serve as a mirror for the recognition of each character's true self.

<u>Shakespeare</u> *demonstrates* how temptation and the supernatural invokes an irreversible change in character, **SUBVERTING** the audience's expectations as he *implies* that a person's poor qualities are amplified by the crown and supernatural. Macbeth becomes paranoid, but the weird sisters simply reveal his true self, as a killer.

In the beginning of the play, Macbeth is *conveyed* as the epitome of a <u>loyal and quintessential Scottish soldier</u> when the Sergeant recalls Macbeth's noble actions as he **"carv'd the passage"** to the traitor Madcdonwald. Specifically, the emotive verb **"carv'd"** carries strong **connotations** of combative expertise and <u>nobility</u>. Alternatively, it could* *allude* to him carving his name famously in the beginning of the play and eventually notoriously at the end of the play, **FORESHADOWING** his drastic moral decline. The stark **CONTRAST** between Macbeth murdering an enemy of the king (**<u>which would be seen as an enemy to God due to the Divine Right of Kings believed by the contemporary audience</u>**) and when he commits <u>regicide</u> - *emphasises* that this murder is the ultimate <u>sin</u>.

Macbeth echoes the witches' equivocation in Act 1 Scene 3 "**so fair and foul a day I have not seen**". By this point in the play, Macbeth had not yet met the witches which could* *allude* to some form of supernatural power the witches have over Macbeth. Alternatively, Shakespeare could* be *suggesting* that Macbeth is already evil and corrupt and his demise is destined due to his **"vaulting ambition"**.

There is no proof <u>Shakespeare</u> had any belief in the supernatural, but he certainly had a **<u>motive to flatter King James I as he was his patron and the financier behind Shakespeare's company</u>** "The King's Men". Therefore, he allows us to *interpret* the witches as either controlling Macbeth, or simply exposing his true nature. <u>Shakespeare</u> therefore creates AMBIGUITY surrounding the supernatural within the play which perhaps* *alludes* to their lack of power and control.

In fact, in Act 1 Scene 3, Macbeth says **"chance may crown me//Without my stir"** with the verb **"stir"** alluding to himself. The witches *show* he can be crowned **"without"** any action from himself, *suggesting* that Macbeth recognises he does not need to do anything to become king. Yet he kills Duncan anyway because of his **"vaulting ambition which o'erleaps itself and falls on th'other"**. A **DACTYLIC METER** is used in this quote which is *reminiscent of* the sound of a galloping horse, perhaps* *suggesting* the relentlessness of Macbeth's ambition: a persistent driving force that is only catalysed by the manipulation of the witches and Lady Macbeth.

The witches' power appears* only to be deception. This is exemplified at the end of the play when Macbeth says **"And be these juggling fiends no more believed"**. The gerund **"juggling"** in this sense *means* trickery and *alludes* to the deception of the witches in manipulating him to his demise by capitalising on his <u>hamartia</u>. The **"fiends"** are what <u>Shakespeare</u> wants the audience to see the supernatural as - nothing more than deceitful game players. Perhaps* he wishes <u>James I</u> would also realise this, but he cannot say this explicitly as he might be executed for witchcraft.

Despite the witches' prophecy of **"for none of woman born shall harm Macbeth"**, Macbeth is slain by Macduff and, although he was born by caesarean, he is technically still born from a woman. Perhaps*, Shakespeare is *hinting* at Macbeth's true killer being his **"vaulting ambition"** and corruption of power, but he continues to paint this with AMBIGUITY to flatter the king with the possibility* of witchcraft, while attacking ambition to warn **the watching nobles against rebellion**.

In conclusion, the supernatural are dependent on the person they are acting upon. Macbeth's violence was already evident before he met the witches when the sergeant described Macbeth's steel as "**smoked with bloody execution**" and the witches simply catalysed the inevitable. However, Banquo was faced with a similar prophecy and yet is **SYMBOLIC** of the route Macbeth didn't take. He is the **ANTITHESIS** to Macbeth's **tragic hero**, and consequently he **ENDED** with the **long-lasting lineage of descendants on the throne**. As **King James I was believed to have been a descendant of Banquo**, Shakespeare ensures to *portray* him in a morally virtuous and positive light to continue **his flattery of the king**, and to *show* the nobility the virtue of not giving in to ambition.

Overall, Shakespeare presents the true crux of the play as temptation and hides this behind the **FACADE** of the supernatural to appease the king. Temptation's relationship with each of the characters differs slightly, but when Macbeth and Lady Macbeth succumb, Shakespeare *uses* their mental decline to ruin every pleasure of usurping the throne, and he *uses* their violent and shameful deaths as a **CAUTIONARY TALE** against sacrificing one's **Christian soul** for ambition.

1074 words

- **Thesis Statement Yes**
- **Explanations 23**
- **Quotes 13**
- **Named Methods 18**
- **Society/era/patriarchal/Jacobean/contemporary/ historical reference etc 16**
- **Shakespeare 10**
- **Exploratory Could, Might, May, Perhaps, Probably 9**
- **Conclusion Yes**
- **Paragraphs 12**

Events:
Perhaps you will be surprised to see that this essay, despite its length, still only concentrates on 6 events.

1. The witches at the start
2. Macbeth is a noble killer at the beginning
3. This foreshadows his identity as a killer of Duncan and his moral decline
4. Macbeth's doubts about killing Duncan despite his vaulting ambition
5. Macbeth's reaction to the witches at the end
6. Contrast to Banquo's reaction to the witches

My Comments

This is typical of the essays students send me. It is typical of the essays I used to get when I was in the classroom. In a top set of 30, at least 9 would write this well, and 5 would write a lot more.

That meant even the laziest student in the class was writing 750 words.

I am sure an examiner would say this is 'beyond GCSE', which it probably is. But that does not mean it should be.

What are the techniques which make a difference?

It's the ones I've listed all the time in this guide:

Write as much as you can, as though a T Rex is chasing you and the only way to slow it down is to feed it words. 900 – 1200 words.

- **Thesis Statement Yes** – set it out in 3 parts and write about Shakespeare's purpose
- **Explanations 23** – write as many as you can
- **Quotes 13** – 13 to 15 and zoom in on individual words
- **Named Methods 17** – name every time you use a quote if you can, and include terms about structure
- **Society/era/patriarchal/Jacobean/contemporary/ historical reference etc 16** – weave them in like embedded quotes to prove your point
- **Shakespeare 10** – keep coming back to Shakespeare's purpose – easy to link to his methods
- **Exploratory Could, Might, May, Perhaps, Probably 9** – use tentative language to show you are writing an 'exploratory response'.
- **Conclusion Yes** – link to Shakespeare's purposes again.

These are 8 skills you need to develop.

Most of you won't be able to do them as well as this essay. That is not the point!

All of you can get better at each of these and dramatically improve your grade. Which means *most* of you can genuinely get at least a grade 7. Go back and look at the grade 7 answers to see what I mean.

ChatGPT

ChatGPT is improving all the time. At the time of writing, it is good enough to get a grade 8.

It can't yet do this on its own, but by combining paragraphs and organising them in chronological order, you can get a pretty good essay.

Here is the essay, with ChatGPT's marking. It is probably accurate to within 1 mark. Examiners only have to be accurate within 3 marks!

My Final Version Combining ChatGPT Paragraphs

Response 26

Shakespeare's *portrayal* of Macbeth as a violent character in Macbeth serves as a **CAUTIONARY TALE**, showcasing the consequences of unchecked ambition and regicide within **the Jacobean context**, warning against the destructive nature of unbridled ambition.

In this extract the Captain vividly *portrays* Macbeth's actions during the recent battle against the Norwegian invaders, *presenting him* as a highly skilled and ruthless warrior. The Captain's description, however, **FORESHADOWS** Macbeth's propensity for violence throughout the play, revealing why Shakespeare *presents* Macbeth as a violent character.

Firstly, Macbeth is *depicted* as an exceptional warrior, skilled in combat and unyielding in the face of adversity. The Captain compares the intensity of the battle to "**two spent swimmers that do cling together**". This **SIMILE** *highlights* Macbeth's tenacity and determination, showcasing his readiness to engage in brutal conflicts.

Moreover, the Captain describes Macbeth's killing Macdonwald, so that Macbeth "unseam'd him from the nave to the chops". The word choice of "**unseam'd**" *implies* a violent and precise act of cutting open the enemy's body, underscoring Macbeth's willingness to inflict gruesome harm.

Furthermore, as Macbeth plans the murder of King Duncan, he contemplates the violent act by stating, "**I have no spur/To prick the sides of my intent, but only/Vaulting ambition**". The **METAPHOR** of a "spur" *conveys* the idea of motivation or justification for violence, *implying* that Macbeth's ambition alone drives him to commit heinous acts.

Similarly, when Macbeth contemplates the consequences of his violent actions, he exclaims, "**Will all great Neptune's ocean wash this blood/Clean from my hand?**". The **METAPHOR** of "Neptune's ocean" *emphasises* the magnitude of guilt and the impossibility of washing away the bloodshed, *highlighting* Macbeth's realisation of the irreversible consequences of his violent deeds.

In contrast to his initial portrayal as a valiant warrior, Macbeth becomes increasingly ruthless in his pursuit of power. After ordering the murder of his loyal friend Banquo, Macbeth remarks, **"To be thus is nothing, but to be safely thus"**. The emphasis on being "**safely**" *indicates* Macbeth's willingness to resort to violence to ensure his own security, even if it means betraying those closest to him.

In another instance, Macbeth contemplates his own resolve and determination, saying, **"From this moment/The very firstlings of my heart shall be/The firstlings of my hand"**. The **REPETITION** of "**firstlings**" *emphasises* Macbeth's readiness to act violently and impulsively, as his thoughts are immediately translated into violent deeds. This impulsive nature *indicates* that Macbeth's immediate response to his desires or intentions is to resort to violent actions. By linking the "**firstlings**" of his heart with the "**firstlings**" of his hand, Macbeth *implies* that violence is his instinctive and primary response to any situation, *underscoring* his inclination towards aggression and bloodshed.

Additionally, when faced with the news of his wife's death, Macbeth reflects on the futility of life, exclaiming, **"Life's but a walking shadow, a poor player/That struts and frets his hour upon the stage"**. The **IMAGERY** of a "**walking shadow**" and a "**poor player**" *conveys* a sense of nihilism and insignificance, *suggesting* that Macbeth's violent actions have stripped life of its meaning and value.

For instance, when reflecting on his past, Macbeth remarks, **"I have almost forgot the taste of fears"**. The phrase "**taste of fears**" *suggests* that Macbeth has become desensitized to fear and violence, indicating his deep immersion in a world of brutality. The **METAPHORICAL** use of "**taste**" *implies* that Macbeth has become accustomed to fear, *implying* a familiarity with violence that has eroded his capacity for empathy or remorse.

Moreover, <u>Shakespeare</u> presents Macbeth as a <u>**CAUTIONARY TALE within the Jacobean context**</u>. The play serves as a warning to <u>**dissuade the nobles from committing regicide**</u>, an act considered <u>**treasonous and disruptive to the established social order**</u>. Macbeth's violent actions and his subsequent downfall *illustrate* the devastating consequences of unchecked ambition and the disruption it brings to <u>**the natural order**</u>.

In conclusion, <u>Shakespeare</u> *presents* Macbeth as a violent character driven by ambition, skilled in combat, and plagued by psychological turmoil. The portrayal of Macbeth's violence, as seen in the imagery of unseaming bloodshed and ambition, *reveals* the darker aspects of his character. Moreover, the play's cautionary nature and its exploration of the <u>**consequences of regicide underscore the moral message of the Jacobean era**</u>. Macbeth's journey from a valiant warrior to a tyrant consumed by violence and guilt exemplifies the <u>tragic</u> consequences of yielding to one's darkest impulses.

722 words

- **Thesis Statement Yes**
- **Explanations 22**
- **Quotes 9**
- **Named Methods 6**
- **Society/era/patriarchal/Jacobean/contemporary/ historical reference etc 7**
- **Shakespeare 3**
- **Exploratory Could, Might, May, Perhaps, Probably 0**
- **Conclusion Yes**
- **Paragraphs 12**
- **Words per paragraph 60**

My Comments

These numbers suggest that this essay would score at the top of Level 5 and therefore gain 25 marks.

ChatGPT Comments

Based on the AQA GCSE literature mark scheme, I would assign this essay a score of 27 out of 30. Here is the justification for the marks:

1. Content: The essay demonstrates a strong understanding of the play and effectively explores Macbeth's violent character, his motivations, and the consequences of his actions. It discusses key scenes and quotes that support the analysis. (Score: 9/10)

2. AO2: Language and Structure: The essay effectively uses quotations from the play to support its arguments. It identifies and analyses literary techniques such as simile, metaphor, and repetition, highlighting their impact on character development and thematic exploration. The essay is well-structured, presenting a clear introduction, body paragraphs organized by theme, and a concise conclusion. (Score: 9/10)

3. AO3: Context and Interpretation: The essay demonstrates an understanding of the Jacobean context and how it influences the play's themes and messages. It discusses the cautionary nature of Macbeth within this context, warning against regicide and the disruption of the social order. The interpretation of Macbeth's journey and the exploration of the consequences of unchecked ambition are insightful. (Score: 9/10)

4. Technical Accuracy: The essay exhibits a strong command of language with effective use of vocabulary and terminology relevant to literary analysis. The writing is clear and coherent, showcasing an ability to convey ideas and arguments effectively. There are minimal grammatical errors or issues with sentence structure. (Score: 9/10)

Overall, the essay provides a well-structured and insightful analysis of Macbeth's violent character, supported by relevant evidence from the play. It demonstrates a strong understanding of literary techniques and contextual factors.

This is very interesting. Let's see how accurate it is. I copied in response 18, worth 26 marks, and asked ChatGPT to grade it.

Assessment Objective 1: Understanding of the text (10/10)

The essay demonstrates a strong understanding of the text, particularly in relation to Lady Macbeth's portrayal as a character consumed by guilt and her manipulation of Macbeth. The analysis accurately identifies key scenes and quotes that support this interpretation.

Assessment Objective 2: Analysis of the text (9/10)

The analysis of the text is mostly effective, providing insightful interpretations of key quotes and techniques used by Shakespeare. The essay explores the repetition of "Out, damned spot" as emphasizing the effects of the spilled blood and the symbolic representation of the "spot" as a mark of evil. The use of monosyllables and dramatic irony is also discussed to highlight Lady Macbeth's psychological struggle.

Assessment Objective 3: Contextual understanding (8/10)

The essay demonstrates an understanding of the Jacobean context, particularly in relation to beliefs about witches and the societal roles of women. The references to Lady Macbeth's desire to adopt a male role and the portrayal of her power being shocking to a Jacobean audience show contextual awareness. However, further elaboration and specific examples could enhance the contextual analysis.

27 marks

This illustrates how marking is still subjective.

Both ChatGPT have tried to mark using a numerical scoring system.

Our marks, of 25 and 26, are both right, as long as we are not further than 3 marks away from the senior examiner.

So, marks of 24, 25, 26, 27 and 28 would all be acceptable.

I don't make the rules!

Printed in Great Britain
by Amazon